cooking with
YORKSH
RAPESEED OIL

Recipes by Angie Boyer and Jennie Palmer
with contributions from Esther Palmer and Jason Thompson

Design and Production by Paul Boyer
Photography by Paul Boyer and Jennie Palmer
with contributions from Alex Oates, Tony Bartholomew
and Jason Lowe

First published in 2014 by
PSB Design & Print Consultants Limited
P.O. Box 5, Driffield YO25 8JD

Copyright © PSB Design & Print Consultants Limited 2014

ISBN: 978-1-873847-03-9

Printed in the UK by Warners Midlands plc

A selection of hand crafted ceramics have been used in the images, made by:
Northumbrian Craft Pottery, Chris & Geoff Cox, David Hilton, Pollie & Garry Uttley,
Rob Watson, Francoise Dufayard, George Ormerod, Jan Burgess, Kushi Grazzini.

For Charlie & Ivy
So that they will know what it was all about

Our Thanks

We first talked about producing a book about Cooking with Yorkshire Rapeseed Oil many months ago, then the idea gradually started to take shape and become a real project. So we'd like to say a big thank you to everyone who has helped to make our idea a reality...

Adam and Jennie, Ben and Esther (Adam's parents) and all the team involved with producing, selling and marketing Yorkshire Rapeseed Oil, without those amazing people and products there would be no book!

To James Mackenzie for writing the Foreword, and to him and our other Guest Recipe writers, Justin Staal, Mary and Steve Anstey and The Chilli Jam Man (Simon!) all of whom gave their valuable time and knowledge to contribute to the book.

A huge thank you to Tracey Baty, three60 marketing and pr, for her meticulous copy checking, what a star!

You all know who you are - our sincere apologies if we've unintentionally missed your name out here - thank you to you all, especially our daughter Jennie, for her enthusiasm and originality in developing recipes, it would have been a different story without her help!

Finally, of course, we'd like to say thank you to you, for delving into this book, we hope you enjoy our recipes!

Angie and Paul Boyer

Contents

All Yorkshire Rapeseed Oil products can be ordered online at **www.yorkshirerapeseedoil.co.uk** or see our website for details of our stockists and the markets we'll be attending.

Foreword

Any chef worth his or her salt these days will tell you that they make every effort to buy their produce locally, make sure it's sustainable, keep a weather eye on air miles – we all know the drill.

What few make claims for on their menus is how important it is to them to work with people they like, trust and can completely depend on. It's something which has always mattered to Kate and me at the Pipe and Glass Inn.

Adam and Jennie Palmer from Yorkshire Rapeseed Oil are key members of that 'circle of trust'.

We've known them since they set their company up in 2008, just two years after the Pipe and Glass opened. They're only a short hop over the Wolds, so we see plenty of them.

Adam and Jennie and their extended family – all of whom seem to be involved in their business one way or another! – are an absolute joy to work with. Their charming children, Charlie and Ivy, are not dissimilar in age to our own pair.

The oil is superlative – their claim that it can be used to 'drip, drizzle, roast, bake, fry' is so much more than just marketing-speak.

And among their excellent range of 'original oils' you'll find one infused with black pepper, inspired by a version I made some years ago to drizzle on our Yorkshire strawberries three ways. If imitation is the sincerest form of flattery – then consider me flattered!

Both images by Tony Bartholomew

James Mackenzie
Michelin Starred Chef
The Pipe & Glass Inn
www.pipeandglass.co.uk

From Small Seeds...

The story of Yorkshire Rapeseed Oil begins in the beautifully unspoilt countryside of the Yorkshire Wolds, where the crops that result in this multi-award winning product are grown and harvested. The magic that nature performs when fields of golden flowers ripen and mature to produce tiny black seeds, happens again at North Breckenholme Farm in Thixendale, when the presses take over and transform the seed into Cold Pressed Extra Virgin Yorkshire Rapeseed Oil.

It sounds idyllic doesn't it - and to be honest, it really is! Thixendale is one of the most gorgeous places imaginable, tucked away in the rolling hills of North Yorkshire, yet only a short drive from the vibrant city of York. Britain's best loved artist, David Hockney, found inspiration in this tranquil area, the place that Adam and Jennie Palmer and their young family have made their home. North Breckenholme Farm has been worked by Adam's family since the early 1950s and it was in 2002 that Adam took it over. Located on the Halifax Estate, the core business had traditionally been arable farming and sheep rearing, but Adam realised that with changing times, diversification was the key to a successful future.

Following extensive research, Adam's original aim was to produce rapeseed oil purely to sell in bulk to large food manufacturers, but sometimes fate takes a hand and presents ideas and opportunities that lead in different directions. Adam's decision to try selling bottled oil at a few local Farmers' Markets transformed his oil production business and now the Yorkshire Rapeseed Oil team can be seen at one or more markets or shows most weekends of the year. Add to that the prestigious trade and public shows that they attend in London, Harrogate and Birmingham, plus stockists across the county and beyond, and you begin to appreciate just how much has already been achieved.

The original natural oil is a firm favourite with customers at the markets and lots of local chefs like to use it too as its high burn point gives them a versatility in their cooking that no other type of oil offers. Yorkshire Rapeseed Oil's distinctive nutty flavour is considered to be a result of the unique qualities of the chalky ground where the rape seed grows. As with a fine wine, the region's soil conditions and climate have a profound influence on the taste of the end product.

But the story doesn't end there, far from it, for an extensive range of flavoured oils, dressings and mayonnaise have all been created using the natural oil as the base. This is a small family business, working a small farm and creating a product which not only has proven health benefits, but also echoes the sentiment that Adam and his wife Jennie have, of supporting and promoting all things local.

The range continues to develop, having progressed from creating new products at the farmhouse kitchen table, to major production on the farm in 'the oil shed' by a team which includes family and friends, the same people who tried and tested the new recipes before they were launched into the market place.

We've all really enjoyed creating these recipes for you and hope they inspire you to experiment for yourself, finding new and exciting ways to use your favourite Yorkshire Rapeseed Oil products in your cooking. *Angie Boyer*

RED RIBBON AWARDS 2014

Pure Gold
because family businesses are priceless

Commended for Excellence

Yorkshire Rapeseed Oil
Extra Virgin Cold Pressed

What does it all mean?

Quite simply, it means the very best quality!

The Oil

'Extra Virgin Cold Pressed' tells you that this is the first, and for us, the only pressing of the rapeseed and that the oil is extracted entirely naturally, there are no additives or chemicals used at all. (If an oil is not cold pressed, it may mean that chemicals have been used to extract more oil from the seed). A large screw-like device is used within the press to squeeze the oil from the rapeseed, producing pure oil that retains all its natural goodness. Our oil is really healthy too, it contains only half the saturated fat and eleven times the Omega 3 of olive oil. It's a great source of the 'healthy' Omegas 3, 6 and 9 too, all in the correct combination to be most beneficial for you and your body.

The Recipes

We are a family that loves to cook, so devising these recipes and ideas for using Yorkshire Rapeseed Oil products has been great fun. We're always mindful of using the best quality ingredients, ethically produced and locally sourced whenever possible, and if they can be organic too, so much the better.

In fact we grow a lot of the vegetables, herbs and fruit that we use in our own kitchen garden, but if you're not able to do that, you might like to try growing some of the things you use most in patio containers or window boxes, it's a real treat to be able to pick fresh salad leaves or ripe, juicy strawberries for a meal.

We hope that our recipes will introduce you to new and different ways of using our products, they're all great to use in the traditional way of course, for cooking, drizzling, dipping or as dressings, but here we show you that they can become much more. Our aim is to inspire you, not to teach you to cook, so nothing is set in stone, often you'll find that you can easily substitute a different Yorkshire Rapeseed Oil product for the one used in the recipe to create interesting and tasty dishes. It's all very versatile and we hope that we've encouraged you to experiment with different ways of using our products yourself!

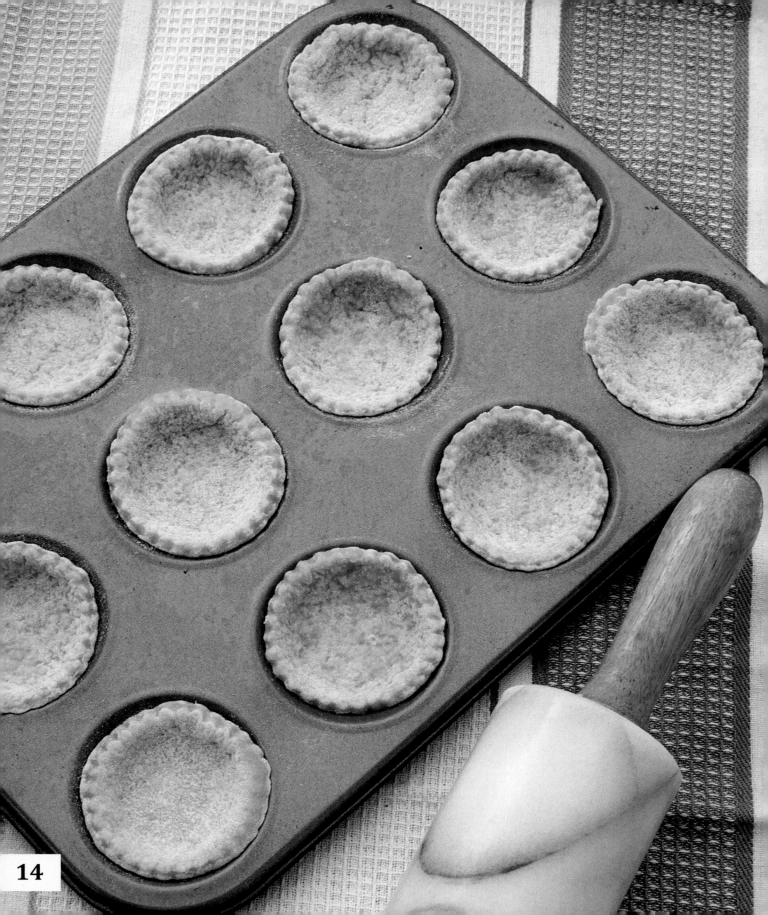

14

Basics

These pastries are dairy free. They're ready to roll out straight away and don't need to be left to rest in the fridge at all.

Beat the Yorkshire Rapeseed Oil and egg together, combine with the flour and gradually add sufficient water to make a soft dough.

Roll out on a lightly floured surface and use for your favourite recipes, setting the oven temperature as required by the recipe you're using.

Try this...

* **Yorkshire Rapeseed Oil with Mixed Herbs** for making pastry for savoury tarts and pies.

Plain Pastry

Makes enough to line a 20cm pie dish or about 16 small tartlets

2¹/₂ tbsp Yorkshire Rapeseed Oil
200g plain flour
1 egg
3-4 tbsp cold water

Mix the flour and sugar together. Beat the Yorkshire Rapeseed Oil and egg together, combine with the flour and sugar mix and gradually add sufficient water to make a soft dough.

Roll out on a lightly floured surface and use for your favourite recipes, setting the oven temperature as required by the recipe you're using.

Try this...

* Use **Yorkshire Rapeseed Oil with Lemon** for making pastry for fruit tarts and pies

Sweet Pastry

2¹/₂ tbsp Yorkshire Rapeseed Oil
200g plain flour
50g caster sugar
1 egg
3-4 tbsp cold water

Pizza Dough

Makes 2 large pizza bases

1tbsp Yorkshire Rapeseed Oil
320g strong white flour
(plus extra for rolling out)
$1/2$ tsp salt
1 tsp sugar
Half a 7g sachet fast action dried yeast
150ml warm water

For Pizza Dough
Preheat the oven to 230ºC / Fan 210ºC / Gas Mark 8

Using a food mixer with a dough hook, mix together the flour, salt, sugar and yeast on a slow speed. Add the Yorkshire Rapeseed Oil and the water and mix for 5 minutes on a higher speed to create a soft, smooth dough.

Leave in a warm place until doubled in size. Remove from the bowl and knead it gently back to its original size. Cut the dough in half and shape each piece into a ball. Using a rolling pin on a surface lightly dusted with strong flour, roll the dough out into a large thin round shape.

Place the pizza base on a round baking tray and cover with your favourite topping. Bake for about 10 minutes until the base is crispy and the top is cooked through.

Try this...
* Spread a layer of **Basil and Pine Nut Pesto** on the base before adding mozarella cheese, quartered artichoke hearts, sliced mushrooms and anchovy fillets.
* Spread a layer of **Rich Roasted Tomato Sauce** on the base before adding scrunched up slices of prosciutto, slices of onion and tomatoes, and crumbled Yorkshire Blue cheese.
* Brush the base with our **Smoked Chilli Dressing** before adding grated mozzarella and slices of chorizo, tomato and red onion.
* Use our **Yorkshire Rapeseed Oil with Lemon** to make the base, with a topping of asparagus, parmesan and mozzarella, plus a little Lemon Oil drizzled over.
* Make the dough using one of our **Original Oils** for a flavoured pizza base.

For Bread

Preheat the oven to 230°C / Fan 210°C / Gas Mark 8

Line two 20 x 10cm loaf tins with baking paper.

Using a food mixer with a dough hook, mix the flour, salt and yeast together on a slow speed. Add the Yorkshire Rapeseed Oil and about 400ml of the water. Mix until combined and then gradually add as much of the remaining water as you need to make a soft dough. Mix on a higher speed for 5 minutes.

Remove the dough from the bowl and turn onto a surface that's lightly dusted with strong flour. Knead the dough back to its original size and cut into two halves. Shape each piece to fit a loaf tin and leave in a warm, draught free place to rise until doubled in size. (Fast action dried yeast requires only one rising of the dough).

Bake for about 30-35 minutes. To test whether the loaf is cooked, using oven gloves remove it from the tin and tap it on its base, the bread should sound hollow when it's cooked through.

Try this...

* This bread freezes really well, either leave the loaf whole, or slice and freeze it so that you can defrost just as much as you need at a time.

* For a crispy crust, brush the top of the loaf before baking it with **Yorkshire Rapeseed Oil** or any of our **Original Oils** of your choice.

Bread

Makes 2 loaves

25g Yorkshire Rapeseed Oil
750g strong flour, white or wholemeal
(plus extra for kneading into shape)
1 x 7g sachet fast action dried yeast
2 tsp salt
450ml warm water

For Flatbread

Combine all the ingredients in a mixing bowl until a dough starts to form, then turn out onto a floured surface.

Bring together into a ball and divide into six pieces. Using a well floured rolling pin (this dough can be quite wet), roll out each piece until it is about 12cm diameter and a few millimetres thick. Place each piece on a plate using baking paper to separate.

Heat a griddle pan on a high heat on the hob until it is hot then cook each flatbread, one at a time, for a few minutes on each side. Griddle marks will form and the bread will start to puff up slightly when cooked.

Great served with dips!

Try this...

* **Lemon and Tarragon Flat Bread** - make the dough using **Yorkshire Rapeseed Oil with Lemon** and add 1 tbsp chopped, dried tarragon to the mixture.

* **Oak Smoked Oil and Rosemary Flat Bread** - use **Oak Smoked Oil** to make the dough and add 1 tbsp dried rosemary to the mixture.

Flatbread

Makes 6

2 tbsp Yorkshire Rapeseed Oil
250g low fat natural yogurt
250g plain flour (plus extra for rolling out)
1 tsp baking powder
A pinch of salt

Always use dried herbs, as fresh ones will burn on the griddle.

17

Both of these sponges can be used for cake and pudding recipes. This quantity is enough for 2 x 20cm circular cake tins, which should be cooked at 200°C / Fan 180°C / Gas Mark 6 for about 20-25 minutes.

Put all the ingredients into a large mixing bowl and beat together well until they form a golden batter.

Cook according to the recipe you are using.

Sponge

120ml Yorkshire Rapeseed Oil
55ml milk
175g self raising flour
175g caster sugar
3 large eggs

Dairy Free Sponge

175ml Yorkshire Rapeseed Oil
175g self raising flour
175g caster sugar
3 large eggs

Preheat the oven to 200°C / Fan 180°C / Gas Mark 6

Grease a 20cm tart/flan tin.

Make the pastry according to the instructions on page 15.

Roll the pastry out on a floured surface and place in the tart/flan tin, trimming any overhanging edges. Prick the base with a fork, place a piece of baking paper cut to size onto the pastry base, cover with baking beans and blind bake for 15 minutes. Remove from the oven when the sides start to crisp, remove the baking beans and paper, ready to add your filling.

Whilst the pastry is baking, heat the oil for your filling in a large frying pan or wok. Add the onions and fry on a medium high heat until they start to soften. Sprinkle over the sugar and balsamic vinegar and continue to fry until the vinegar has reduced down and the onions are soft. Remove from the heat ready for filling your tart.

In a bowl beat together the cream and eggs and season well.

Now add the filling to your partly cooked pastry case. Spread the onions evenly over the base. Then scatter over the Yorkshire Blue cheese, pushing some of it into the onions. Finally, pour over the egg mixture and make sure all the onions are evenly coated.

Place back in the oven for 30 minutes or until the filling is firm.

Serve warm or cold with a summer salad drizzled with our **Mint and Balsamic Dressing**.

Red Onion and Yorkshire Blue Tart

One quantity of Pastry (see page 15)

For the Filling
3 tbsp Yorkshire Rapeseed Oil
4 red onions, peeled and finely sliced
3 tbsp Balsamic vinegar
2 tsp golden caster sugar
100g Yorkshire Blue cheese, cut into 1cm cubes
150ml double cream
5 medium eggs
Salt and pepper to season

A delicious combination of chicken and vegetables under a crisp pastry topper.

Preheat the oven to 200°C / Fan 180°C / Gas Mark 6

Make the pastry according to the instructions on page 15 and set aside until needed.

Heat the oil in a pan on a high heat and fry the onion, chicken and bacon until the chicken starts to brown, stirring continuously. Add the butternut squash and keep stirring for another 3 or 4 minutes. Then add the leek, mushrooms and garlic. Stir and turn the mixture over a high heat for another couple of minutes then add the wine. Allow to reduce over a high heat for 5 minutes then sprinkle the flour over the mixture. Stir the flour through then slowly add the stock, stirring thoroughly, until a sauce starts to form. Turn the heat down to low and cook gently while you roll out the pastry.

Roll the pastry out on a floured surface to a size and shape slightly larger than the pie dish.

Put the chicken mixture in to the pie dish, brush the beaten egg around the edges of the filled dish and then cover with your pastry topper. Trim and pinch the edges to hold the pastry in place and make some small holes in the top to release the steam when cooking. Use any trimmings for decorating the top of the pie crust.

Finally brush the pastry with the remaining beaten egg and place in the oven. Cook for 25-30 minutes until the pastry is golden.

Delicious served with steamed green vegetables and **Honey and Mustard Mash.**

Chicken, Bacon and Butternut Squash Pie

One quantity of Pastry (see page 15)

For the filling
2 tbsp Yorkshire Rapeseed Oil
1 onion, peeled and finely chopped
200g free range chicken breast, diced
3 rashers British bacon, cut into strips
250g butternut squash, peeled, seeded and chopped into 2cm cubes
100g (1 medium) leek, chopped
50g chestnut mushrooms, quartered
2 garlic cloves, peeled and crushed
3 tbsp plain flour
100ml dry white wine
300ml good chicken stock
1 egg, beaten

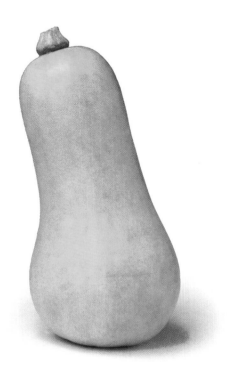

The quantities shown here make a big pan full, so be sure to either use a good sized pan or halve the quantities when you make this. It freezes brilliantly and the relatively long cooking time (along with the addition of red wine!) creates a rich Bolognese-style sauce that even non-veggies seem to enjoy. Serve with your favourite pasta or in a lasagne.

Vegetarian 'Bolognese' style Pasta Sauce

Makes a big pan full!

3 tbsp Yorkshire Rapeseed Oil
1 large onion, peeled and chopped
4 sticks celery, thinly sliced
2 carrots, peeled and sliced
225g chestnut mushrooms, sliced
2 garlic cloves, peeled and crushed
400g tin chopped plum tomatoes
2 tbsp tomato puree
275ml vegetable stock
275ml red wine
450g packet meat free vegetarian mince
1 tbsp chopped fresh herbs (e.g. parsley, thyme, marjoram) *or* 1tsp dried mixed herbs
2 bay leaves

Heat the Yorkshire Rapeseed Oil in a large pan and fry the onion until soft. Add the celery and carrots and cook for 2-3 minutes more over as medium heat, turning frequently. Add the mushrooms and garlic and cook for another 5-10 minutes more over low heat to soften all the vegetables, stirring from time to time.

Now add the vegetarian mince, herbs and bay leaves. Mix well and then add the tin of tomatoes, tomato puree, vegetable stock and wine. Bring to the boil, mix well, turn the heat down to low, cover the pan and simmer gently for one and a half hours, stirring occasionally to prevent sticking.

Try this...
* Stir in cooked kidney beans and generous amounts of our **Yorkshire Rapeseed Oil with Chilli** for a **Veggie Chilli Non-Carne.**
* **Vegetarian Moussaka -** slice up an aubergine, brush with **Yorkshire Rapeseed Oil with Garlic** and griddle on both sides until starting to brown. Do the same with 2 or 3 sliced courgettes. Then slice up a couple of large cooked potatoes. Layer potato, courgette, 'Bolognese' style sauce and aubergine in an ovenproof dish. Top with a layer of thick white sauce that's had 3 eggs beaten into it and a packet of Feta cheese crumbled in.
Bake in the oven at 200°C / Fan 180°C / Gas Mark 6 for about 1 hour until the top is golden and has set.

Rich Roasted Tomato Sauce

6 tbsp Yorkshire Rapeseed Oil
1 kg tomatoes
A good handful of fresh basil leaves
6 fat cloves of garlic, peeled and
roughly chopped
Freshly ground black pepper

When tomatoes are plentiful, roast and then blitz them for a rich tomato sauce that's packed with flavour. Freeze it in small quantities and defrost to use for pizzas, stir into fresh pasta, or add to soups and casseroles for a reminder of that wonderful summer taste.

Preheat the oven to 200°C / Fan 180°C / Gas Mark 6

Roughly tear up the basil leaves and scatter them across the bottom of a large, shallow oven proof dish. Cut the tomatoes in half - about a kilo, but a few more or less will be fine - and place them cut side up in a single layer on top of the basil leaves. Peel the cloves of garlic, chop them roughly and scatter over the tomatoes. Season with black pepper. Drizzle the Yorkshire Rapeseed Oil over the tomatoes.

Bake for about an hour, until the edges of the tomatoes are beginning to blacken.

Remove from the oven and set aside to cool. Then put into a liquidiser, scraping every last bit from the dish. Blitz to create a rich roasted tomato sauce.

Try this...
*Add our **Smoked Chilli Dressing** to the tomatoes when you blitz them for a spiced-up version of the sauce - add a little at a time and taste as you go for the flavour that suits you.

Quick & Easy Tomato and Lentil Soup

Serves 8

3 tbsp Yorkshire Rapeseed Oil
2 onions, peeled and chopped
2 x 400g tins chopped tomatoes
1 litre vegetable stock
100g dried split red lentils
Salt and pepper to season

This tasty soup takes only minutes to make using ingredients found in most kitchen cupboards

Rinse the red lentils in a sieve under running cold water until the water runs clear. Drain well.

Heat the Yorkshire Rapeseed Oil in a large pan and fry the chopped onions until soft and translucent. Add the tomatoes, stock and lentils. Bring to the boil, stirring constantly, turn the heat to low, cover the pan and simmer for 25 minutes until the lentils are cooked, then blitz/liquidise. Season with salt and pepper to taste.

Serve with **Herb Toast**
Lightly toast both sides of thick, chunky slices of bread, then brush one side of each slice with **Yorkshire Rapeseed Oil with Mixed Herbs** and put under the grill for a couple of minutes to crisp.

Try this...
* **Summer Soup** - add a good dash of **Yorkshire Rapeseed Oil with Chilli** or a larger dash of **Smoked Chilli Dressing** and serve the soup ice cold.
Cool but with a kick!

Justin Staal
Staal Smokehouse
www.staalsmokehouse.co.uk

"We were lucky enough to meet Justin Staal of Staal Smokehouse at a tasting a few years ago, when the Smokehouse was first setting up. Since then our paths have crossed at many markets and foodie events and it seemed the perfect collaboration when we wanted to create a smoked oil." **Jennie and Adam Palmer.**

Place the lamb on a work surface, meat side down, and score the skin side of it.

In a bowl or dish large enough to take all the ingredients, mix the Yorkshire Rapeseed Oil and white wine. Add the juice and zest of the oranges, lemons and lime. Crush the garlic and add to the bowl together with the rosemary, thyme, salt and pepper plus the chopped chillies if you are using them.

Mix the marinade thoroughly and then add the lamb. Massage the lamb well with the marinade and then cover and place in the fridge for a minimum of 12 hours, longer if you want a more intense flavour.

To cook the lamb, fire up the barbecue, if you are using charcoal make sure that the coals are placed to one side. Remove the lamb from the marinade and lay it flat on the barbecue to sear, first one side and then the other. After searing the meat, place it on the side away from the coals and cook for 20 minutes on each side.

Let the lamb rest for 20 minutes then carve and serve.

GUEST RECIPE

Marinated Barbecued Lamb

500ml Yorkshire Rapeseed Oil
1 leg of lamb that has been butterflied
(ask your butcher to do this if you're not sure how)
250ml white wine
1 whole bulb of garlic
2 oranges, juice and zest
2 lemons, juice and zest
1 lime, juice and zest
Sprigs of fresh rosemary and thyme
Salt
Cracked black pepper
2 whole chillies (optional)

29

Our Plain Oatcakes are wheat and dairy free.

Preheat the oven to 190ºC / Fan 170ºC / Gas Mark 5

Put all the dry ingredients into a large bowl and mix together well. Pour in the Yorkshire Rapeseed Oil and then the boiling water – add the water a little at a time, to ensure that the mixture doesn't become too wet. (Add a little more oatmeal if it does).

Using a palette knife, draw all the ingredients together, combining them thoroughly, then form into a ball of soft dough using your hands.

Roll the dough out on a surface dusted with fine oatmeal and cut into rounds with 6cm round pastry/biscuit cutter.

Gather and reroll the trimmings, the mixture can dry out and become crumbly quite quickly, so work a little more hot water into it if this happens, to soften it again.

Place the oatcakes on baking tray lined with baking paper and bake for 20 minutes until crisp, turning them over after 10 minutes so that they cook evenly on both sides. Remove from the oven and leave to cool on a wire rack.

Try this...
* Use **Yorkshire Rapeseed Oil with Mixed Herbs** and add 50g grated mature cheddar cheese for yummy **Cheese and Herb Oatcakes.** You'll need to use less water, about 4 tbsp, so add that gradually to get the right consistency.

Plain Oatcakes

Makes approx 20 oatcakes

2 tbsp Yorkshire Rapeseed Oil
225g fine oatmeal
½ tsp baking powder
6-7 tbsp boiling water

Sweet Oatcakes

Simply add 50g soft dark brown sugar to the Plain Oatcake recipe and follow the same method instructions.

Try this...
* Add 50g stem ginger, drained from the syrup and finely chopped, to the Sweet Oatcakes recipe and use **Yorkshire Rapeseed Oil with Ginger** for **Ginger Oatcakes.**

A gorgeous cake for sunny summer afternoon teas - with a very indulgent filling!

Preheat the oven to 200°C / Fan 180°C / Gas Mark 6

Grease 2 x 20cm circular cake tins and dust them with self raising flour.

Make the sponge according to the instructions on page 19.

Divide the mixture evenly between the two sponge tins and bake until cooked through, a skewer inserted into the centre of the sponge should come out clean - usually about 20/25 minutes. Cool the sponges slightly before removing from the tins and placing on a wire rack until cold.

For the filling, whip the cream and then carefully fold in the fruit and crushed meringues. Be sure that the sponges are completely cold before spreading raspberry jam on each of them and then sandwiching them together with the filling.

Dust the top with icing sugar to finish.

Try this...
* Add crumbled white or dark chocolate for an even more indulgent filling!

Classic Victoria Sponge with an Eton Messy Middle

For the sponge:
One quantity of either regular or dairy free sponge mixture (see page 19)

For the filling:
450ml double cream
175g fresh strawberries, roughly chopped
50g fresh blueberries
50g fresh raspberries
3 meringue nests, crushed

To finish:
Raspberry jam
Icing sugar

Preheat the oven to 170°C / Fan 150°C / Gas Mark 3

Grease and line 2 x 20cm circular cake tins.

Combine all the cake ingredients in a mixing bowl and beat together until a smooth batter is formed. Pour the batter into the prepared cake tins, splitting equally between them both.

Place in the oven and cook for 20-25 minutes or until cooked. A skewer inserted into the middle of the cake should come out clean if it is cooked.

Leave to rest for a few minutes then remove from the tins and cool on a wire rack.

When the cakes are cooled, whip the double cream until firm, adding the icing sugar just at the end of whipping. Firstly spread the jam generously over one of the cakes, followed by the cream. For a bit of extra luxury, scatter in the chocolate chips if using them, then place the second cake on top.

Dust with Icing sugar to finish.

Dark Chocolate Cake with a Blackberry Jam Middle

For the Cake
170ml Yorkshire Rapeseed Oil
175g plain flour
50g Green & Black's cocoa powder
1 heaped tsp baking powder
1 heaped tsp bicarbonate of soda
2 tbsp treacle
2 eggs
75g golden caster sugar
120ml milk

For the filling
150g blackberry jam
200ml double cream

To finish:
2 tsp icing sugar
A handful of chocolate chips (optional)

A seriously scrumptious sticky treat!

Pre heat the oven to 180°C / Fan 160°C / Gas Mark 4

Line an 20 x 30cm shallow baking tin with baking paper.

Warm the sugar, syrup and Yorkshire Rapeseed Oil together in a large saucepan over a medium heat. Add the oats and mix thoroughly. Remove from the heat.

Put the chopped figs with the orange juice and zest into a small pan and mix together over a low heat for 4 or 5 minutes, stirring continuously. Remove from the heat.

Spread half of the oat mixture in the base of the baking tin. Spread the fig and orange mixture on top of that. Cover with a layer of the remaining oat mixture.

Mark into 16 pieces with a knife. Bake for 20-25 minutes, until golden on top. Remove from the oven.

Mark the 16 pieces again with a knife, leave in the tin until cold then turn out and separate into flapjacks

Try this...
* Use **Yorkshire Rapeseed Oil with Ginger** for a tangier taste.
* Ring the changes by using different dried fruits, such as ready-to-eat dried apricots.
* Add chopped nuts for a crunchier texture.

Makes 16

170ml Yorkshire Rapeseed Oil
110g light brown sugar
75g golden syrup
350g porridge oats
225g 'Ready to Eat' dried figs, any stalks removed, then roughly chopped
Juice and grated zest of 1 orange

Image Alex Oates

Preheat the oven to 190°C / Fan 170°C / Gas Mark 5

Grease and line a 20cm circular cake tin.

Sift the flour into a mixing bowl and stir in the sugar and almonds. Add the Yorkshire Rapeseed Oil, milk, vanilla essence, almond essence and eggs. Mix thoroughly until you have a smooth batter. Add the apples to the batter and stir through.

Pour the mixture into a the cake tin and bake for about 45 minutes or until cooked through. A skewer inserted into the middle should come out clean when the cake is cooked.

Cool slightly before turning out onto a wire rack. When cold, decorate with a dusting of icing sugar and flaked almonds before serving.

Almond and Apple Cake

180ml Yorkshire Rapeseed Oil
140g golden caster sugar
100g ground almonds
150g self raising flour
½ tsp vanilla essence
½ tsp almond essence
3 eggs, beaten
80ml milk
2 small eating apples, peeled, cored and cut into chunks
50g toasted flaked almonds
Icing sugar for dusting

40

A deliciously light loaf that's easy to make and perfect served with a good cup of tea!

Apple and Raspberry Loaf

Preheat the oven to 190°C / Fan 170°C / Gas Mark 5

Line a 20 x 10cm loaf tin with baking paper

Put the sugar, flour, Yorkshire Rapeseed Oil, milk, baking powder and eggs into a bowl and beat well until they form a golden batter.

Put about a quarter of the batter into the loaf tin and then place half of the apple on top.

Put a further quarter of the batter in the tin and scatter the raspberries on top.

Place a further quarter of the batter on top of the raspberries and add the remaining sliced apple.

Top with remaining batter and cook in the oven for approximately 1 hour 10 minutes until fully cooked - a skewer inserted into the middle should come out clean when the loaf is cooked.

Serve warm or cold with crème fraîche, custard or ice cream - or just by itself!

Try this...
* This cake is good made with any seasonal fruit, especially rhubarb, which works well if you slice it up and put it in the microwave for a minute or two to soften slightly before adding it to the batter in the tin.

120ml Yorkshire Rapeseed Oil
175g golden caster sugar
55ml milk
3 eggs
175g self raising flour
1 tsp baking powder
1 large cooking apple, peeled, cored and finely sliced
1 small handful (about 75g) of fresh or frozen raspberries

A favourite with Charlie when he's cooking with his Mum, these little pudding pots are great for children to make with the help of an adult - and the adults enjoy eating them just as much as the children do!

Preheat the oven to 200°C / Fan 180°C / Gas Mark 6

Grease 4 ramekin dishes.

Core and chop the apples and put them in the ramekins.

Make the cake batter by putting the flour, sugar, Yorkshire Rapeseed Oil, milk and egg into a bowl and beating all the ingredients together well.

Pour the batter over the apples in the ramekin dishes.

Sprinkle with a dusting of cinnamon and bake in the oven for 20-25 minutes until the sponge is cooked through.

Charlie's Pudding Pots

Makes 4

50ml Yorkshire Rapeseed Oil
2 eating apples
100g self raising flour
100g golden caster sugar
1 medium egg, beaten
50ml milk
Dusting of cinnamon

The lightly toasted crunchy walnuts complement the smooth, rich coffee and cream flavour of this ice cream perfectly.

Coffee and Walnut Ice Cream

1 tbsp Yorkshire Rapeseed Oil
100g walnuts, broken into fairly large pieces
570ml double cream
6 egg yolks
175g golden caster sugar
8 tsp strong instant coffee
(Instant Espresso is ideal)

Check the capacity of your ice cream maker and halve the quantities given here if necessary.

Mix the instant coffee with a little boiling water to dissolve it. Leave to cool.

Whisk the egg yolks and sugar together in a bowl until thick and pale cream in colour.

Put the cream into a non-stick pan over a low to medium heat and warm until just below boiling point, stirring continuously. Pour the warmed cream over the egg and sugar mixture in the bowl and mix well. Add the cooled coffee mixture and whisk thoroughly.

Cover the bowl with cling film and leave to cool. When cool, place in the fridge to chill.

Meanwhile heat the Yorkshire Rapeseed Oil in a frying pan, add the walnuts and turn continuously until browned or 'toasted' all over. This only takes a couple of minutes, so take care not to burn them. Remove from the pan, drain on kitchen paper and leave to go cold.

When the ice cream mixture is chilled, add the toasted walnuts and pour into the ice cream maker, churning until thick and frozen. Remove and put into a suitable container before storing in the freezer until ready to serve.

Try this...
* Toast some extra walnut pieces and lightly salt them to nibble with drinks!

Serving Tip...
*After churning in the ice-cream maker, put portions of ice cream into cappucino coffee cups along with a wafer roll and then freeze. Be sure your cups are freezer proof though!

45

Ben Palmer

Yorkshire Rapeseed Oil Original Range

Our Original Oils are recommended for use as high quality cooking, drizzling and dipping oils. When our Yorkshire Rapeseed Oil is flavoured, the herbs and spices remain in the bottle, intensifying the flavour more over time. These flavours transfer superbly into your cooking when heated and are great when used as rubs and marinades.

Chilli and Spice
Our Yorkshire Rapeseed Oil has been marinated with a mix of chilli and spices to create a full flavoured yet mild cooking oil.

Black Pepper
The combination of our Yorkshire Rapeseed Oil and cracked black pepper has created a beautiful flavour that's fantastic for frying steaks, adding a kick to pasta sauces and casseroles or even just spicing up a salad.

Mixed Herbs
Our Award Winning Yorkshire Rapeseed Oil has been marinated with a delicious mix of herbs to create a fabulous earthy flavour to suit all seasons. Great for dipping bread, drizzling on fresh pasta or when cooking your Sunday roast.

Hot and Spicy Pumpkin and Lentil Soup

Big, fat, orange pumpkins abound in October, the shops stacking them high ready for Halloween creative carvings. They're brilliant to grow too – almost expanding before your very eyes! But what to do with so much pumpkin, especially when it can sometimes end up being a bit watery when cooked? We make batches of this thick and warming soup and freeze it, ready for those cold winter days, it's excellent served with Pumpkin & Walnut Bread.

Serves 6

2 tbsp Yorkshire Rapeseed Oil with Chilli and Spice
1-2 tsp Yorkshire Rapeseed Oil with Chilli
1 large onion, peeled and chopped
350g pumpkin flesh, (peeled weight), cut into small pieces
850ml hot vegetable stock
110g dried split red lentils, rinsed in a sieve under running cold water until it runs clear
1 tsp ground cumin
1 tsp ground coriander
$1/2$ tsp turmeric
Salt and pepper

Using a large saucepan, fry the onions in the Yorkshire Rapeseed Oil with Chilli & Spice over a gentle heat until soft. Add the pumpkin and cook over medium heat for another couple of minutes, stirring continuously.

Add the lentils, stock, cumin, coriander and turmeric. Bring to the boil gradually over a medium heat, then put a lid on the pan, turn the heat down to low and simmer for about 30-40 minutes until the lentils are cooked and the pumpkin is tender.

Blitz/liquidise, season with salt and pepper and then add Yorkshire Rapeseed Oil with Chilli to flavour, according to your taste.

Try this...
* **Hot and Spicy Carrot and Lentil Soup** - if pumpkins are out of season, this recipe works equally well if you use carrots instead.

49

Pheasant can sometimes be a bit dry, but this method of cooking helps to keep it moist and tender, whilst the chorizo and paprika lend a tasty piquancy to the flavour.

Pheasant with Chorizo and Bacon

Serves 4

3 tbsp Yorkshire Rapeseed Oil with Chilli and Spice
2 pheasants, each cut into 2 leg and
2 breast joints, skin removed
150g piece of chorizo, outer skin removed
and cut into 3mm slices
4 unsmoked British back bacon rashers,
cut into 1cm strips
2 onions, peeled and chopped
4 large tomatoes
3 fat cloves of garlic, peeled and
finely chopped
4 tbsp dry white wine
150ml beef stock
1 tbsp tomato purée
1-2 tbsp plain flour
2 bay leaves
1 tsp paprika

Preheat the oven to 170ºC / Fan 150ºC/ Gas Mark 3

To remove the skins from the tomatoes: place them in a heat proof bowl, cover with boiling water and leave for a couple of minutes until the skins have split. Carefully drain away the hot water and when cool enough to handle, peel off the skins.
Cut the tomatoes into quarters and remove and discard the seeds.

Roughly chop the remaining tomato flesh.

Using a deep frying pan or wok on a hot hob, heat 2 tbsp of the Yorkshire Rapeseed Oil with Chilli and Spice and fry the chopped bacon until crispy. Remove the bacon from the pan and put into an ovenproof casserole dish which has a lid.

Roughly chop half the chorizo slices (leave the other half to one side for the garnish), put into the frying pan and cook until the fat has been released and the chorizo is crispy. Remove from the pan and add to the bacon in the casserole.

Coat the pheasant joints in the flour and cook in the frying pan to brown and seal the meat. Remove and add to the casserole with the bacon and chorizo.

Fry the onions and garlic in the same frying pan until just beginning to brown. Then add the chopped tomatoes, dry white wine, beef stock, tomato purée, bay leaves and paprika. Stir well over the heat to mix everything together. When the mixture starts to bubble, pour it into the casserole over the meat. Cover with a tight fitting lid and cook in the oven for 30 minutes.

Meanwhile, heat the remaining 1tbsp Yorkshire Rapeseed Oil with Chilli & Spice in a frying pan and fry the remaining chorizo until crispy. Remove the chorizo from the pan and drain it on kitchen paper, ready to use as a garnish.

Season the casserole with salt and pepper to taste and serve the pheasant (a leg and a breast joint per person) with the chorizo and bacon sauce and a crispy chorizo garnish.

Try this...
* **Chicken with Chorizo and Bacon** - chicken joints may be used instead of the pheasant, in which case the cooking time in the oven may need to be extended a little.

Peel and cook the potatoes, drain and put into a mixing bowl and then mash them with 1tbsp of the Yorkshire Rapeseed Oil with Chilli and Spice.

Prepare the cabbage by cutting it in half, removing the inner stalk and any thick ribs in the leaves, then shred finely. Heat 3 tbsp of the Yorkshire Rapeseed Oil with Chilli and Spice in a wok and add the cabbage. Stir fry over a high heat, stirring and turning constantly, for about 4-5 minutes, until the cabbage has reduced in volume by about half and is just starting to brown at the edges.

Put the cabbage into the bowl with the potato and mash everything together until well mixed. Divide into 6 even sized portions and shape each one into a flat round about 2cm thick.

Heat a small amount of Yorkshire Rapeseed Oil with Chilli and Spice in a frying pan and shallow fry the Bubble and Squeak cakes, first on one side and then the other, until brown and crispy.

Meanwhile fry the eggs, either in natural Yorkshire Rapeseed Oil or Yorkshire Rapeseed Oil with Chilli and Spice, whichever you prefer and place on top of the Bubble and Squeak to serve.

Spicy Bubble and Squeak with a Fried Egg Topper

Makes 6

4 tbsp Yorkshire Rapeseed Oil with Chilli and Spice plus extra for frying
750g potatoes (mashed weight roughly 550g)
500g Savoy cabbage
6 eggs

A very easy to make, versatile salad that's good as a side dish with curries, or as part of a barbecue salad buffet.

Heat the oils together in a wok or frying pan over a high heat. Add the black mustard and cumin seeds, stir and remove the pan from the heat as soon as the seeds start to pop. Stir in the turmeric, lemon juice and a pinch of salt. Add the grated carrots and mix well. Turn into a serving bowl and chill before serving.

Carrot Salad

1 tbsp Yorkshire Rapeseed Oil with Chilli and Spice
1 tsp Yorkshire Rapeseed Oil with Garlic
225g carrots, peeled and grated
$1/2$ tsp black mustard seeds
$1/2$ tsp cumin seeds
$1/4$ tsp ground turmeric
1 tbsp lemon juice
Salt to taste

Cook the rice according to the instructions on the packet and then drain in a colander or sieve.

Meanwhile, mix the cream, cumin and turmeric together.

Heat the Yorkshire Rapeseed Oil with Black Pepper in a wok over a high heat on the hob. Add the onion and fry until golden.

Turn the hob down to medium and add the cooked rice to the pan and mix well over the heat.

Fold in the cream and spice mixture, the sultanas and almonds, turning to mix well over the heat.

Gently fold in the cooked flaked fish and 2 tbsp chopped fresh coriander.

Add the wine a little at a time, carefully turning the mixture in the pan on the hob to heat everything thoroughly.

Serve garnished with the quartered eggs and the remaining coriander.

Creamy Smoked Haddock Kedgeree

Serves 4

2 tbsp Yorkshire Rapeseed Oil with Black Pepper
600g smoked haddock, cooked, skin and bones removed and broken into fairly large flakes
225g basmati rice
1 onion, peeled and chopped
200ml double cream
4 tbsp chopped fresh coriander
50g sultanas
25g flaked almonds
3 tsp ground cumin
1 tsp ground turmeric
6-8 tbsp dry white wine
4 hard boiled eggs, shells removed and cut in half

Preheat the oven to 220°C / Fan 200°C / Gas Mark 7

Using a food mixer with a dough hook, first add the flour to the bowl then the salt and yeast (add each to different sides of the bowl so they do not mix immediately). Then add the Yorkshire Rapeseed Oil with Black Pepper and the water.

Mix on a slow speed for 5-10 minutes until the dough is formed. This dough is very wet so keep your surfaces and hands well floured when handling.

To test if it is ready, make a ball with the dough then, using a well floured finger, prod a shallow indent in the side. If the dough springs back then it is ready to shape. If the not, knead for a few minutes longer.

When the dough is ready, form it into an oval shape and place on a well floured baking try. Cover with oiled cling film and leave to rise for about 1 hour or until the dough has doubled in size.

When the dough has risen, remove the cling film and use your finger to push holes into it, placing snippets of the rosemary into the holes, then sprinkle with some sea salt.

Bake in a hot oven for about 25–30 minutes, or until the bread is well risen and sounds hollow when tapped underneath.

Allow to cool. Once cooled but still warm drizzle over a little more of the Yorkshire Rapeseed Oil with Black Pepper and then slice, ready to serve.

Black Pepper and Rosemary Focaccia

80ml Yorkshire Rapeseed Oil with Black Pepper, plus extra for drizzling
500g strong white flour, plus extra for dusting
$1^1/_2$ tsp salt
1 x 7g sachet fast action dried yeast
270ml warm water
A few sprigs of fresh rosemary
Large pinch of sea salt

Fry the onion in the Yorkshire Rapeseed Oil with Black Pepper in a pan over a medium heat until soft but not brown.

Add the celery to the onion, mix well and cook gently for a few minutes more.

Add the potatoes to the pan. Pour in the stock and bring to the boil.

Cover and simmer gently for about 30 minutes.

Blitz/liquidise until smooth and serve.

Celery Soup

Serves 6

2tbsp Yorkshire Rapeseed Oil with Black Pepper
1 head of celery, washed and thinly sliced
1 large onion, peeled and chopped
225g potatoes, peeled and cut into small pieces
850ml hot vegetable stock

57

We've used fillet steak in this recipe, but the sauce tastes just as good if you prefer a different cut such as sirloin.

Steak with Creamy Black Pepper and Mushroom Sauce

Serves 2

Take the steaks out of the fridge about 30 minutes before you want to cook them.

Cook the thinly sliced onions in the Yorkshire Rapeseed Oil with Black Pepper in a frying pan over a high heat for 2 minutes stirring constantly, until they soften. Turn the heat down to medium and add the mushrooms to the pan. Continue frying and stirring for 3 more minutes, then turn the heat back up to high and add the steaks to the pan.

Cook the steaks on both sides according to your preference, an approximate guide depending on the thickness of the steaks:
Blue = 1 minute on each side
Rare = 2$\frac{1}{2}$ minutes on each side
Medium rare 3 - 3$\frac{1}{2}$ minutes on each side
Well done 4 - 5 minutes on each side

Remove the steaks from the pan and place on serving plates. Take the pan off the hob and add the double cream, stirring to warm through and mix with the mushrooms and onions. Pour the sauce over the steaks and drizzle a little Dijon and Black Pepper Dressing over the mushrooms before serving.

To serve: we've served our steak with **Spicy Bubble and Squeak,** it goes really well with our **Garlic New Potatoes** too!

2 tbsp Yorkshire Rapeseed Oil with Black Pepper
Dijon and Black Pepper Dressing to drizzle
2 fillet steaks, each weighing about 150g
1 small onion, peeled and sliced
100g white baby button mushrooms
4 tbsp double cream

59

Preheat the oven to 170°C / Fan 150°C / Gas Mark 3

Peel the potatoes and cut them into slices about 1cm thick. Place the slices in the bottom of an ovenproof casserole dish.

Heat the Yorkshire Rapeseed Oil with Mixed Herbs in a frying pan or wok over a moderate heat and brown the lamb shanks, one at a time. Turn them frequently to ensure that the meat is browned and sealed all over. As you remove each one from the pan, place it on top of the potato slices in the casserole dish.

Add the sliced onions to the pan after all the lamb has been removed and cook over a high heat, stirring and turning constantly until turning brown.

Add the garlic to the onion in the pan and cook for a minute or two more. Roughly chop the tomatoes after removing the skins and seeds (see page 51) and add to the pan. Season with salt and pepper.

Pour the vegetables over the lamb shanks in the casserole dish, crumble the feta cheese on top and cover tightly with either a lid or foil.

Cook for 1 hour and then turn the oven down to 150°C / Fan 130°C / Gas Mark 2 and cook for one more hour. When cooked, the meat should almost fall away from the bone and the potatoes will be full of the flavours of the meat and sauce.

Slow Cooked Lamb Shanks

4 tbsp Yorkshire Rapeseed Oil with Mixed Herbs
4 British lamb shanks
2 onions, peeled and sliced
2 cloves garlic, peeled and chopped
2 tomatoes, skins and seeds removed, (see page 51)
3 large potatoes
2 packets Feta cheese
Salt and black pepper

Fry the onion gently in the Yorkshire Rapeseed Oil with Mixed Herbs over a medium heat until soft but not brown. Remove from the heat, put into a blender or food processor. Drain and roughly chop the artichoke hearts and add to the onion, along with the wine vinegar. Blitz/liquidise until smooth and serve with lots of tasty bread to scoop and dip!

Artichoke Dip

2tbsp Yorkshire Rapeseed Oil with Mixed Herbs
390g tin of artichoke hearts in water (240g drained weight)
1 small onion, peeled and finely chopped
1 tsp white wine vinegar

Preheat the oven to 200°C / Fan 180°C / Gas Mark 6

Line two 20 x 10cm loaf tins with baking paper.

Use a food mixer with a dough hook attachment for this recipe.

Grate the pumpkin and put it into the bowl of the food mixer with the walnuts, flour, dried yeast and salt, mix well together. Add the Yorkshire Rapeseed Oil with Mixed Herbs and most of the water and mix on a slow/medium speed into a soft dough, adding more water as necessary. Do not over mix the dough or the pumpkin will release its juices and make the dough too sticky.

Remove the dough from the food mixer bowl and divide it in half. Knead each piece into shape to fit the tins, place into the tins, brush the tops with a little more Yorkshire Rapeseed Oil with Mixed Herbs and leave in a warm but draught free place to rise. When the dough has roughly doubled in size, to fill the tin, place the tins in the centre of the oven and bake for about 35 minutes. To test if a loaf is cooked, using oven gloves remove it from the tin, tap the bottom lightly and if cooked through it should have a hollow sound to it.

Place on a wire rack to cool.

This bread freezes brilliantly, so we make lots of loaves during the pumpkin season and then enjoy them throughout the rest of the year.

Try this...
* Make small individual rolls - the method is the same, they just won't need to cook for quite as long as a loaf in a tin.

Pumpkin and Walnut Bread

Makes 2 loaves

2 tbsp Yorkshire Rapeseed Oil with Mixed Herbs plus a little more to brush on the top of the loaves
750g strong white flour
100g walnuts, roughly chopped
300g pumpkin flesh, prepared weight after skin and seeds removed
1 x 7g sachet fast action dried yeast
1 tsp salt
250ml tepid water (approx)

Slow cooking, red wine and the aromatic qualities of Yorkshire Rapeseed Oil with Mixed Herbs turns a relatively inexpensive cut of beef into something rather delicious! You can use braising/stewing steak cut into chunks instead of the joint of Brisket if you prefer.

Preheat the oven to 170C / Fan 150C / Gas Mark 3

Coat the beef in plain flour. Heat the Yorkshire Rapeseed Oil with Mixed Herbs in a wok or frying pan over medium heat and add the beef. Turn frequently so that all of the meat is browned. Remove the beef from the pan and put it into an ovenproof casserole dish which has a lid.

Fry the bacon in the pan until it releases the fat and becomes crisp. Remove from the pan with a slotted spoon and add to the beef in the casserole dish.

Now add the onions to the pan and cook over medium heat until they begin to soften. Add the mushrooms and garlic. Continue to cook, turning frequently, for 3 minutes. Remove the vegetables from the pan with a slotted spoon and add to the beef and bacon in the casserole dish.

Mix any remaining flour (from coating the meat) with a little of the red wine. Add the mixture to the oil and fat residues remaining in the pan, stirring constantly. Gradually pour in the rest of the wine and the beef stock, stirring thoroughly. Bring to the boil and then carefully pour over the beef and bacon in the casserole dish. Add the bay leaves, season with salt and pepper, cover with a lid and cook in the middle of the oven for 30 minutes.

Then turn the oven down to 150°C / Fan 130°C / Gas Mark 2 and cook for another hour.

Remove from the oven and slice the beef joint before serving with the sauce.

Excellent with **Honey and Mustard Mash**!

Beef Braised in Red Wine

Serves 4

2 tbsp Yorkshire Rapeseed Oil with Mixed Herbs
Brisket of beef joint weighing approximately 1kg
3 tbsp plain flour
4 rashers British streaky bacon, cut into thin strips
2 onions, peeled and sliced
250g small mushrooms
2 garlic cloves, peeled and crushed
2 bay leaves
200ml beef stock
500ml red wine
Salt and pepper to taste

Yorkshire Rapeseed Oil.
Grown and produced in and around the village of Thixendale on the Yorkshire Wolds

Yorkshire Rapeseed Oil Deli Range

A smaller bottle ideal for gifts and hampers. Our flavoured oils within this range are made by combining our cold pressed Yorkshire Rapeseed Oil with a drop of essential oil, creating a clean pure flavour. They are great as culinary oils, ideal for frying, roasting, dressing and dipping.

Basil

A lovely light flavour, ideal for making pesto and bruchetta. Drizzle on fresh pasta, or tomato and mozzarella salad.

Chilli

Ideal for adding heat to your cooking. Great for stir-fries, or use to spice up casseroles, soup or pasta dishes.

Garlic

Ideal for cooking fish and seafood, or simply to roast potatoes. Drizzle onto pizzas or use as a frying base to inject a great flavour into your cooking.

Ginger

Perfect for stir-frying, this subtly flavoured oil works wonders with Thai dishes, it adds a certain something to puddings as well.

Lemon

Fantastic for cooking fish and chicken and delightfully refreshing drizzled on a summer salad, great to use in baking too!

Oak Smoked

Our Two Gold Star Award Winning Yorkshire Rapeseed Oil has been expertly smoked to a secret recipe by Staal Smokehouse to create a delicious cooking oil ideal for dressings, drizzling and roasting.

Smoked Salmon and Leek Tagliatelle in a Parmesan Basket

Simple to make, but impressive enough in appearance for a special dinner party!

To make the parmesan baskets, preheat the grill to high. Place one of the paper circles on the grill pan and spread 30g of grated parmesan over it to within about 1cm of the edge all round. Leave gaps in the cheese, so that it will create a lace effect when melted.

Place under the hot grill until the cheese is bubbling and beginning to crisp and turn brown.

Remove from the grill and carefully place the sheet of melted cheese over the top of a breakfast cereal bowl. Using the end of the handle of a wooden spoon, gently push the centre of the sheet of melted cheese down into the bowl, creating a bowl or basket shape with the cheese.

Refrigerate until needed. When ready to serve, carefully peel the cheese and paper apart to reveal each parmesan basket.

To make the Smoked Salmon and Leek Tagliatelle, thinly slice the leeks, wash and drain well. Cut the smoked salmon into 1cm strips. Heat the Yorkshire Rapeseed Oil with Lemon in a wok and cook the leeks gently over low heat until soft but not brown. Add the smoked salmon strips and stir continuously until the fish has cooked through. Now add the soured cream, still stirring, until everything is heated through. Season with a few twists of black pepper.

Meanwhile cook the tagliatelle according to the instructions on the packet. Drain well and add to the leek and salmon mixture in the wok. Mix everything together carefully but thoroughly before dividing between the four parmesan baskets to serve.

Try this...
Fill your Parmesan baskets **Prawn and Mushroom Tagliatelle**, with a touch of **Smoked Chilli Dressing** stirred into the soured cream.

Serves 4

For the Parmesan Baskets
Make the Parmesan baskets well in advance. For each basket you will need 30g coarsely grated parmesan cheese plus a circle of baking paper about 23cm in diameter and a breakfast cereal bowl.

For the Smoked Salmon and Leek Tagliatelle
3-4 tbsp Yorkshire Rapeseed Oil with Lemon
4 large leeks (prepared weight about 600g)
250g smoked salmon
300ml soured cream
400g fresh egg tagliatelle
Black pepper

Lemon and Lime Rice

Serve with Spiced Chilli Chicken, Spicy Chick Peas and Minted Yogurt

Cook the rice according to the instructions on the packet and drain.

Heat the Yorkshire Rapeseed Oil with Lemon in a wok over high heat. Add the well drained rice and lime zest. Turn and toss the rice until it's all coated in the oil. Add the lime juice, stirring and turning well to mix thoroughly before serving.

Try this...
Use cold as the base for a **Rice Salad,** adding cold, cooked mixed vegetables such as peas, sweetcorn, sliced green beans, or perhaps diced black olives, capers, pumpkin seeds and roughly chopped sundried tomatoes.

Serves 4

2 tbsp Yorkshire Rapeseed Oil with Lemon
250g Basmati rice
2 limes – grated zest and juice

Broad Bean Dip

This works well with broad beans that are a bit older and have started to go floury. If you don't have fresh broad beans, frozen beans are fine to use.

Cook the beans, allow to them cool and then remove the outer coating, keeping just the green inner bean - a bit of a fiddly job, but quite therapeutic!

Put all the ingredients into a blender and blitz into a smooth paste. Serve with warm flatbread.

Try this...
* Use **Honey & Mustard Dressing** instead of the Yorkshire Rapeseed Oil with Black Pepper
* **Green Pea Dip** - substitute peas for beans and use **Mint and Balsamic Dressing** instead of the Yorkshire Rapeseed Oil with Black Pepper

1 tbsp Yorkshire Rapeseed Oil with Lemon
1 tbsp Yorkshire Rapeseed Oil with Black Pepper
450g broad beans (shelled weight)
Salt to taste

Yorkshire Rapeseed Oil is brilliant for deep frying as it has a high burn point and by frying the chips twice, you get a wonderful golden colour and a really crunchy texture. You would expect to use old potatoes for chips, but we have found that the 'Accord' new potatoes that we grow in our vegetable garden make surprisingly good chips - so try different types and see what you find!

Start by deep frying the chips in the Yorkshire Rapeseed Oil, 10 minutes for fat chips, 5 minutes for matchstick sized 'frites'. Remove the chips from the oil and leave them to cool for at least 20 minutes. Take the oil off the heat.

When you're ready to finish cooking the chips, reheat the Yorkshire Rapeseed Oil and deep fry the them again for about 10 minutes until crisp and golden. Remove and drain, serve with a sprinkling of salt.

To prepare the mussels, clean them by scraping away the 'beard' from the base of the shell and discarding any which are open and do not close when you tap them, or which have damaged shells. Rinse them in cold water and drain well.

Using a deep pan large enough to hold the mussels when their shells have opened, gently fry the onion in the Yorkshire Rapeseed Oil with Lemon until translucent. Add the tomatoes, herbs, a few twists of black pepper and the wine and heat until simmering.
Tip in the mussels, cover with a lid and cook over high heat for a few minutes until the shells have opened, shaking/turning a couple of times to mix the mussels into the sauce. Be careful not to overcook the mussels, or they could become tough, and do not eat any which have not opened. Serve with Twice Fried Chips - and the rest of the bottle of white wine!

Mussels 'Provencal' style with Twice Fried Chips

Serves 1 as a main course or 2 as a starter

1tbsp Yorkshire Rapeseed Oil with Lemon Yorkshire Rapeseed Oil for deep frying
Potatoes, peeled, cut into chips and dried
1kg mussels
1 onion, peeled and finely sliced
2 tomatoes, peeled and seeds removed, remaining flesh chopped (see page 51)
1 tsp dried Herbes de Provence
Freshly ground black pepper
4 tbsp dry white wine

73

Preheat the oven to 190ºC / Fan 170ºC / Gas Mark 5

Grease a 20cm tart/flan dish.

Make the pastry according to the instructions on page 15, roll it out on a lightly floured surface and line the flan dish with it. Prick the base with a fork, cover with a circle of greaseproof paper cut to size, put some baking beans on top of the paper and blind bake it in the oven for 10 minutes. Take out of the oven, remove the baking beans and paper and leave to one side, ready for the filling to be added.

To make the filling, mix the blackcurrants, lemon zest and sugar together in a bowl. Mix the cornflour to a smooth paste with the lemon juice, add to the fruit in the bowl and mix thoroughly.

Pour the fruit mixture into the pastry case, drizzle a small amount of Yorkshire Rapeseed Oil with Lemon over the fruit and cook in the oven for about 35 - 45 minutes until the pastry is cooked and the fruit mixture has set.

Serve warm with cream or ice cream.

Blackcurrant and Lemon Tart

One quantity of Sweet Pastry made with Yorkshire Rapeseed Oil with Lemon (see page 15)

Yorkshire Rapeseed Oil with Lemon to drizzle

500g blackcurrants, any stalks removed

2 tbsp cornflour

125g sugar

5 tbsp lemon juice

Finely grated rind / zest of 1 lemon

Preheat the oven to 200ºC / Fan 180ºC / Gas Mark 6

Line a baking tray with baking paper.

Mix the flour, salt and thyme together in a bowl. Add the Yorkshire Rapeseed Oil with Lemon and the milk and mix everything together to form a soft dough. Turn the dough out onto a floured surface and pat it out with your hands until it's about 2cm thick.

Using a 6cm pastry cutter, cut out rounds and place them on the lined baking tray. Gather and reroll the trimmings to make more scones.

Brush the top of each scone lightly with milk and bake in the oven for about 20 minutes until risen and golden. Remove from the oven and place on a wire rack to cool before serving.

Lemon and Thyme Scones

Makes 6

60g Yorkshire Rapeseed Oil with Lemon

250g self raising flour

1 tsp dried thyme

$^1/_4$ tsp salt

130ml milk plus extra for glazing

The Cross Keys Thixendale

The Cross Keys in Thixendale was our first ever stockist and we're proud to say that they still stock and use Yorkshire Rapeseed Oil products today to create some great pub grub!

"We use Yorkshire Rapeseed Oil for frying and salad dressing and of course the chilli and garlic oils are good stock items to have for the basis of tasty pasta or rice dishes - you don't need a lot to glamorise something mundane! We also offer garlic, chilli or natural oil on the couscous accompanying the tagine that we serve, which people enjoy.

"Of course I fry with Yorkshire Rapeseed Oil too and really like the fact that it's very clean, it doesn't leave a nasty coating baked on the fryers as blended oils do... I hate doing the fryers!

Yorkshire Rapeseed Oils are now classed as a staple part of my food store!"

Mary and Steve Anstey
The Cross Keys
Thixendale

To read more about Thixendale and The Cross Keys, visit the village website www.thixendale.org.uk

GUEST TIPS

The variety of ingredients that you can combine to make a Frittata is endless... here are some of our favourites. Served with a crisp green salad, frittata is a meal in itself, it's great served cold for picnics too.

Courgette and Feta Frittata

Serves 4 - 6

1-2 tbsp Yorkshire Rapeseed Oil with Garlic
Mint and Balsamic Dressing
400g courgettes grated
100g feta cheese
5 eggs
75ml milk
Salt and black pepper

Heat the Yorkshire Rapeseed Oil with Garlic in a frying pan with a heat proof handle. Fry the courgettes over a high heat on the hob for 5-6 minutes until cooked through, stirring continuously.

Beat together the eggs and milk with a pinch of salt and a good twist of black pepper. Pour the egg mixture over the courgettes and press down with the back of a spatula to make sure that the whole of the bottom of the pan is covered.

Crumble the feta cheese on top and cook on the hob over a medium heat without touching it for a further 3-4 minutes. Finally, once the base of the frittata seems set, add another twist of black pepper and place the frying pan* under a very hot grill until cooked through.

Serve hot or cold with a drizzle of our Mint and Balsamic Dressing.

*Make sure the frying pan has an heat proof handle!

Try this...
* **Potato, Broccoli, Onion and Cheddar Frittata** using the same method as above with 2 tbsp **Yorkshire Rapeseed Oil,** 1 onion, peeled and chopped, 450g potatoes, peeled and cooked, 110g part cooked broccoli florettes, 150g grated cheddar and 6 eggs.
* Or try this mix of ingredients with your eggs **Red Pepper, Red Onion, Sun Dried Tomato and Black Olive Frittata** using **Yorkshire Rapeseed Oil with Garlic**
* Or maybe this... **Ham, Tomato, Parmesan cheese and Potato Frittata** using **Yorkshire Rapeseed Oil with Black Pepper**

Skin the peppers by cutting each of them into quarters, removing the stalk and seeds and placing them skin side up on a grill pan under a hot grill until the skins blacken. Remove the grill pan from the grill and place a cloth over the peppers for about 30 minutes. Then remove the cloth and the skins should peel off easily.

Slice the skinned peppers into thin strips and put into a bowl. Drizzle a generous amount of Yorkshire Rapeseed Oil with Garlic over the peppers, add a good twist of freshly ground black pepper and some roughly chopped flat leaf parsley. Mix well, cover and leave in the fridge to marinate for at least 2 hours.

To prepare the halloumi cheese, cut it into slices about 1cm thick, dry each slice and coat lightly with plain flour. Heat a small amount of Yorkshire Rapeseed Oil with Garlic in a frying pan over high heat and fry the cheese slices until brown, first on one side and then the other. Remove from the pan and drizzle Mint and Balsamic Dressing over the cheese slices.

Serve the peppers cold with the warm cheese and some fresh, crusty bread.

Try this...
Fried Halloumi with Crispy Bacon - use **Oak Smoked Yorkshire Rapeseed Oil** to marinate the peppers and fry the halloumi, then top the cheese slices with some strips of crispy fried bacon.

Medley of Marinated Peppers with Fried Halloumi

Yorkshire Rapeseed Oil with Garlic
Mint and Balsamic Dressing
1 each of red, yellow and orange sweet peppers
1 packet halloumi cheese
Plain flour
Black pepper
Flat leaf parsley, chopped

Blend all the ingredients except the whole cumin seeds together with either a hand blender or in a food processor. Season to taste with the salt and pepper and serve with a sprinkling of whole cumin seeds on top.

Try this...
Drizzle a little **Yorkshire Rapeseed Oil with Chilli** on top, or **Smoked Chilli Dressing**, for a bit of a kick!

Hummus

4 tbsp Yorkshire Rapeseed Oil with Garlic
200g tin chick peas, drained
Juice of half a lemon
1 tsp ground cumin
2 tbsp water
Salt and black pepper
$1/2$ tsp whole cumin seeds

Preheat the oven to 180°C / Fan 160°C / Gas Mark 4

Cut the aubergine and courgettes into slices about 5mm thick and brush them on both sides with Yorkshire Rapeseed Oil with Garlic. Heat a griddle pan on the hob and when hot, put in a layer of aubergine slices. Cook until griddle marks appear on the underside, turn over and cook in the same way on the other side, then remove from the pan and put to one side on a plate. Cook all the aubergine and courgette slices in this way.

Place layers of the vegetables in a deep ovenproof dish: aubergine, chopped tomato, courgette, chopped tomato, seasoning with salt and pepper as required.

Put the breadcrumbs into a bowl, crumble the feta in on top and mix the two together well. Spread the cheese and breadcrumb mixture over the top of the vegetables, drizzle Yorkshire Rapeseed Oil with Garlic over the top and cook in the oven for about an hour until the top is browned and the vegetables have released their juices.

Aubergine and Courgette Bake

Serves 4

Yorkshire Rapeseed Oil with Garlic
1 aubergine, about 350g
2-3 courgettes, about 500g
1 x 400g tin chopped tomatoes
30g wholemeal breadcrumbs
100g feta cheese
Salt and black pepper

Boil the potatoes until just cooked and drain. Before serving heat the Yorkshire Rapeseed Oil with Garlic in a frying pan and add the potatoes, fry for a few minutes until the skins start to crisp. Serve immediately. This works with other flavoured oils and our **Mint and Balsamic** or **Honey and Mustard Dressings**.

Garlic New Potatoes

Yorkshire Rapeseed Oil with Garlic
New potatoes

First make your meatballs. Peel and quarter the onion and put into a food processor. Tear the bread into chunks and roughly slice the chorizo and add both to the food processor. Blitz until well chopped and breadcrumbs have started to form. Add the egg and Yorkshire Rapeseed Oil with Chilli and then the mince. Continue to blitz on a high speed until a smooth thick paste-like consistency starts to form.

Put the flour into a separate bowl and remove the blade from the food processor. Using your hands shape individual meatballs (about 5cm diameter). When each meatball is formed roll them in the flour and place to one side on a plate ready for cooking. This mix makes around 12 good size meatballs.

When all the meatballs are prepared, cover the bottom of a lidded pan in Yorkshire Rapeseed Oil (enough to shallow fry in). Heat the oil on the hob on a high temperature and when hot, add the meatballs. Fry for about 5 minutes, turning the meatballs to brown them all over. (The aim is to brown the outsides rather than cook through).

Once the meatballs have browned, carefully remove them from the pan and set aside. In the remaining oil make the sauce. Firstly add the onion and fry for a few minutes until soft. Then add the mushrooms and fry a little longer until they start to colour. Then add into the pan the passata, wine and water, season well and add the herbs. Bring the sauce to the boil then carefully put the meatballs in. Try to cover each meatball with a little sauce, but be careful not to handle them to much so they don't lose their shape. Put the lid on the pan, reduce the hob to a low heat and simmer for at least 30 minutes, a little longer if you wish.

When you are near to being ready to serve, cook the fettuccine according to the instructions on the packet and drain. Spoon onto individual plates and serve the meatballs and sauce on top. Finish with a generous grating of parmesan cheese and a drizzle of Yorkshire Rapeseed Oil with Chilli.

Chorizo Chilli Meatballs with Fettuccine

Makes 12 meat balls – Serves 4

For the Meatballs
3 tsp Yorkshire Rapeseed Oil with Chilli
1 onion
1 slice of bread
100g chorizo
1 medium size egg
500g lean steak mince
100g plain flour

For the Sauce
Yorkshire Rapeseed Oil
Yorkshire Rapeseed Oil with Chilli
1 onion, peeled and finely chopped
100g mushrooms sliced
200ml red wine
120ml water
500g tomato passata
1 sprig of fresh rosemary
1 sprig of fresh thyme
Salt and black pepper
250-300g fettuccine pasta (depending on your appetite!)

As with all our Chilli Oil recipes, this dish has a nice warm heat to it. If you would like a more spicy option just add more Yorkshire Rapeseed Oil with Chilli!

Chilli Beef Stir Fry

Serves 2

First prepare the ingredients. Cut the beef and peppers into thin strips, about 1cm thick, and quarter the pak choi. To prepare the spring onions, trim the ends and leave on some green so they are about 8-10cm long, then halve.

Heat the Yorkshire Rapeseed Oil in a wok until hot then add the beef and stir fry for a couple of minutes until it starts to brown. Add the peppers and fry for a few minutes more, then add the spring onions and cook for another 2-3 minutes.

Keeping the wok on the hob at a high temperature, add the cream cheese and stir through. Once it begins to melt, add the milk and stir together until a creamy sauce starts to form.

If you are using dried noodles, now is the time to add them to a pan of boiling water and cook on a second hob.

Return to your wok and reduce the hob temperature to a medium heat allowing the sauce to simmer lightly. Add in the soy sauce and Yorkshire Rapeseed Oil with Chilli and stir through until combined into the sauce then add in the chopped garlic and pak choi. Cook for a further 2 or 3 minutes until the pak choi is tender, but make sure it doesn't over cook.

Drain the noodles and remove the wok from the heat. Combine the noodles into the sauce mix and serve drizzled with a little more Yorkshire Rapeseed Oil with Chilli.

2 tbsp Yorkshire Rapeseed Oil
2 tsp Yorkshire Rapeseed Oil with Chilli, and a little more to serve
300g beef steak
2 pak choi (200g prepared weight)
1 bunch spring onions (75g prepared weight)
1 small red pepper (100g prepared weight)
1 small yellow pepper (100g prepared weight)
80g cream cheese
150ml milk
2tsp dark soy sauce
2 cloves of garlic
150g medium egg noodles

Combine the tomatoes, onion, coriander and lime juice in a bowl. Mix well and the stir in the Yorkshire Rapeseed Oil with Chilli - use more (or less!) to suit your taste.

Chilli Salsa

1 tsp Yorkshire Rapeseed Oil with Chilli
3 large tomatoes, skins and seeds removed (see page 51), remaining flesh chopped
1/2 large red onion, peeled and finely chopped
1 tbsp fresh coriander, chopped
1 tbsp lime juice

Serve these two dishes together with Lemon & Lime Rice and Minted Yogurt. Adjust the flavour to suit your taste with varying amounts of Yorkshire Rapeseed Oil with Chilli.

Spiced Chilli Chicken

Serves 4

Yorkshire Rapeseed Oil with Chilli
3-4 tbsp Yorkshire Rapeseed Oil with Chilli and Spice
4 skinless chicken breasts cut into cubes
2 onions, peeled and thinly sliced
2 tsp ground cumin
2 tsp ground coriander
2 tbsp tomato purée
1 tbsp fresh coriander, chopped
100ml water

Heat the Yorkshire Rapeseed Oil with Chilli and Spice in a wok and add the onion. Fry over a high heat for 2-3 minutes, stirring continuously, until just turning brown. Add the chicken and fry, turning the meat in the pan, for another 2-3 minutes until the chicken is lightly browned.

Now add the ground cumin and coriander and fry for a minute or two more, turning and mixing well in the pan. Add the tomato purée and the water, cover with a lid, turn the heat down to low and cook for about 30 minutes, stirring from time to time to ensure that the chicken doesn't stick to the pan. Remove the lid and add Yorkshire Rapeseed Oil with Chilli to suit your taste. Stir in the chopped fresh coriander before serving.

Spicy Chick Peas and Mushrooms

Serves 4

Yorkshire Rapeseed Oil with Chilli
1 tbsp Yorkshire Rapeseed Oil with Chilli and Spice
1tsp Yorkshire Rapeseed Oil with Garlic
1 onion, peeled and chopped
2 tsp ground coriander
2 tsp ground cumin
1 tsp ground ginger
400g tin chopped tomatoes
450g tin chick peas in water, drained
200g chestnut mushrooms, cut in half
1 tbsp lemon juice
1 tbsp tomato purée

Heat the Yorkshire Rapeseed Oil with Chilli and Spice and Yorkshire Rapeseed Oil with Garlic together in a pan and fry the chopped onion over high heat until golden. Add the coriander, cumin and ginger and fry for a couple of minutes more, stirring continuously. Add the tomato purée, mushrooms, chopped tomatoes, the drained chick peas and lemon juice. Mix well, cover the pan with a lid, turn the heat to low and cook gently for 30 minutes.

Add Yorkshire Rapeseed Oil with Chilli to suit your taste.

Chilli Chocolate Ice Cream

This unusual, but highly moreish ice cream, has echoes of chocolate's Aztec origins, a hint of chilli teasing the palate after the seductively smooth richness of the chocolate. Try it and see, add the oil a teaspoonful at a time, taste as you go to get exactly the right amount of chilli for you, don't be surprised if not all of the mixture makes it into the ice cream maker!

4 tsp Yorkshire Rapeseed Oil with Chilli
275ml full cream milk
275ml double cream
6 egg yolks
110g unrefined caster sugar
150g good quality 70% plain chocolate

Check the capacity of your ice cream maker and halve the above quantities if necessary.

Whisk the egg yolks and sugar together in a large bowl until thick and pale cream in colour.

Put the milk and cream into a non-stick pan. Grate the chocolate and add to the pan. Put over a low to medium heat on the hob and stir constantly so that the chocolate melts into the milk and cream mixture as it warms. Do not allow to boil.

When the chocolate has melted and the mixture is just below boiling point, take it off the heat and pour into the bowl of whisked egg yolks and sugar, stirring continuously.

Whisk or stir until all the ingredients are well combined. Cover the bowl with cling film, leave to cool, then put in the fridge until completely cold.

Remove from the fridge and add the Yorkshire Rapeseed Oil with Chilli, one teaspoonful at a time, mixing thoroughly. Pour the mixture into an ice cream maker and turn until it has thickened and frozen. Remove and put into a suitable container before storing in the freezer until ready to serve.

If you don't have an ice cream maker, pour the mixture into a suitable container and put into the freezer. Remove and break up the mixture with a fork every 20 minutes or so, returning it to the freezer in between stirrings, until it's frozen.

Enjoy!

The sharp, crisp flavour and texture of the Basil and Tomato Salsa contrasts perfectly with the Savoury Prawn Stuffed Pancakes. And fresh basil always seems to release its flavour better if the leaves are torn into small pieces with the fingers, rather than chopped with a blade.

Preheat the oven to 180°C / Fan 160°C / Gas Mark 4

To make the Pancakes
Put the flour, egg and milk into a large jug and mix thoroughly with a hand held blitzer into a smooth, creamy batter. Leave to stand for 30 minutes. Place a 20cm non stick crêpe pan or frying pan, (very lightly greased with Yorkshire Rapeseed Oil if necessary), on a high heat on the hob. When hot, pour in about a sixth of the batter, tilting the pan quickly to spread the mixture out and evenly cover the base. Cook over high heat until set and the underside is lightly browned, this will take only a few moments, then carefully turn the pancake (or toss it, if you're clever!) in the pan and cook the other side. Remove the pancake from the pan and place on a plate.
Cook five more pancakes in the same way.

To make the Filling
Cook the potatoes on the hob in boiling water until tender – about 20 minutes. Drain and leave to cool, then remove and discard the skins. Crush the potatoes roughly with a fork and put to one side.

Fry the onion in 1 tbsp of the Yorkshire Rapeseed Oil with Basil over high heat for about 3 minutes until golden and just beginning to crisp. Remove from the frying pan and place in a large mixing bowl.

Add the remaining 1 tbsp of Yorkshire Rapeseed Oil with Basil to the frying pan and, when hot, add the crushed potatoes. Cook over a high heat, turning frequently, for 5 minutes until the potatoes are just beginning to brown. Remove from the pan and add to the onion in the mixing bowl.

Mix together the yoghurt, lime juice and Honey and Mustard Dressing and add to the potato and onion mixture. Mix well.
Stir in the prawns carefully and finally add the torn basil leaves. Mix thoroughly but gently.

Roughly divide the mixture into 6 portions. Place a portion of the filling across the middle of one pancake and then roll it up into a sausage shape. Make 5 more stuffed pancakes in the same way. Place them all in an ovenproof dish, cover with foil and place in the middle of the oven for 30 - 40 minutes to heat through.

To make the Salsa remove the skins and seeds from the tomatoes (see page 51), then chop the remaining flesh and place into a mixing bowl. Add the onion and stir in the Yorkshire Rapeseed Oil with Basil and the lime juice. Mix thoroughly then stir in the torn basil leaves. Season with a little salt and freshly ground black pepper if you wish.

Remove the stuffed pancakes from the oven and serve with the Salsa.

Savoury Prawn Stuffed Pancakes

Makes 6 stuffed pancakes

For the Pancakes
125g plain flour
1 egg
300ml milk

For the Prawn Stuffing
2 tbsp Yorkshire Rapeseed Oil with Basil
1 tbsp Honey and Mustard Dressing
500g new potatoes, scrubbed clean
250g shelled, cooked prawns
1 medium size onion, peeled and chopped
4 tbsp natural yoghurt
1 tbsp lime juice
1 tbsp fresh basil leaves, torn into pieces

Basil and Tomato Salsa

3 tsp Yorkshire Rapeseed Oil with Basil
6 tsp lime juice
500g tomatoes, skins and seeds removed (see page 51)
1 red onion, peeled and finely chopped
2 tbsp fresh basil leaves, torn into pieces

Preheat the oven to 190°C / Fan 170°C / Gas Mark 5
Grease a 20cm tart/flan dish.

Make the pastry according to the instructions on page 15, roll it out on a lightly floured surface and line the flan dish with it. Prick the base with a fork, cover with a circle of greaseproof paper cut to size, put some baking beans on top of the paper and blind bake in the oven for 10 minutes. Take out of the oven, remove the baking beans and paper and leave it to one side, ready for the filling to be added.

To make the filling, cook the onion in a pan over a high heat in the Yorkshire Rapeseed Oil with Basil until it begins to brown. Remove the onion from the pan and spread over the base of the pastry case. Scatter fresh basil leaves on top of the onion. Cut the tomatoes in half and place on top of the basil and onion, cut side up. Scatter the black olives over the top. Drizzle a little Yorkshire Rapeseed Oil with Basil over the tomatoes and bake in the oven for 35-40 minutes.

Garnish with fresh basil leaves and serve hot or cold.

Roasted Tomato and Basil Tart

One quantity of Pastry made using Yorkshire Rapeseed Oil with Basil (see page 15)

1 tbsp Yorkshire Rapeseed Oil with Basil plus extra to drizzle
350g small tomatoes (approx)
1 red onion, peeled and sliced
8 pitted black olives, sliced
Fresh basil leaves

Place the tomatoes, onion, chopped garlic and 2 tbsp of the Yorkshire Rapeseed Oil with Basil into a bowl, mix well and season with salt and black pepper.

Toast the ciabatta and brush the remaining basil oil on each side, then rub each side of the toast with the halves of garlic.

Spoon the tomato mixture onto the toast and garnish with fresh basil leaves to serve.

Yorkshire Bruschetta

Serves 6

3 tbsp Yorkshire Rapeseed Oil with Basil
4 tomatoes, finely chopped
1 small onion, peeled and finely chopped
1 clove of garlic peeled and halved
2 cloves of garlic, finely chopped
Salt and black pepper to taste
6 thick slices of ciabatta bread
Fresh basil leaves

Pesto is easy to make and wonderful stirred through a bowl of fresh pasta or spread on the base of pizzas. Try mashing it into baked potatoes or stir it into some natural yogurt for a tasty salad dressing. It freezes well, so make lots when basil is fresh and has plenty of flavour.

Put all the ingredients into a food processor and blitz together, or alternatively put into a bowl and use a hand blender. That's all there is to it!

Basil and Pine Nut Pesto

5 tbsp Yorkshire Rapeseed Oil with Basil
1 tbsp Yorkshire Rapeseed Oil with Garlic
50g fresh basil leaves
25g pine nuts
40g grated parmesan cheese
Sea salt

Duck Breasts with Ginger and Orange Sauce and Ginger Garnish

The duck is tender and tasty when served medium rare, but if you prefer your meat a little more well-done, then leave it in the oven for a few minutes longer.

Preheat the oven to 200°C / Fan 180°F / Gas Mark 6

Put an ovenproof dish large enough to hold 4 duck breasts into the oven to heat up.

Heat the Yorkshire Rapeseed Oil with Ginger in a frying pan on the hob and cook the duck breasts, skin side down, over a high heat until the skin is brown and crispy and the fat begins to release into the pan. Turn the duck breasts over and fry on the other side for a couple of minutes to seal and brown the meat.

Remove the duck breasts from the frying pan and place into the preheated ovenproof dish. Cook in the oven for 9 minutes for medium rare meat.

Meanwhile, with the frying pan off the heat, stir the flour into the oil and duck fat remaining in the pan, then gradually mix in the orange juice and zest and green ginger wine. Season with salt and pepper. Return to the hob and gradually bring to the boil, stirring continuously to create a smooth sauce. If the sauce is too thick, add a little water or stock.

To make the Ginger Garnish, fry the slices of bread and the slices of stem ginger in the Yorkshire Rapeseed Oil with Ginger over a high heat, first on one side and then the other, until brown and crispy. Remove from the pan and drain on kitchen paper.

To serve, remove the duck breasts from the oven, slice the meat and place on individual plates with the sauce.

Garnish with the ginger fried bread and slices of fried stem ginger.

Serves 4

1 tbsp Yorkshire Rapeseed Oil with Ginger
4 duck breasts, each weighing approx 200g
1 tbsp plain flour
2 oranges – zest and juice
6 tbsp green ginger wine
Salt and pepper

For the Ginger Garnish
4 tbsp Yorkshire Rapeseed Oil with Ginger
4 thick slices of bread
4 pieces of stem ginger in syrup, drained, dried and thinly sliced.

Plum and Ginger Crunchy Crumble

Preheat the oven to 190°C / Fan 170°C / Gas Mark 5

Wash the plums, cut in them in half and remove the stones, then place them all in an ovenproof dish.

To make the crumble topping, mix the flour, oats, sugar, Golden Syrup and Yorkshire Rapeseed Oil with Ginger together in a bowl until thoroughly combined and then place on top of the plums in the dish.

Cook in the oven for 30-40 minutes until the top is crispy and golden. Serve hot with custard, cream or ice cream.

Serves 6

150ml Yorkshire Rapeseed Oil with Ginger

100g porridge oats

175g plain flour

200g golden caster sugar

100g Golden Syrup

1kg plums

Preheat the oven to 200ºC / Fan 180ºC / Gas Mark 6

Combine all the ingredients except the rhubarb in a mixing bowl and beat together until a sooth batter is formed. Stir in the rhubarb until it is mixed evenly into the batter. Spoon the mixture into the muffin cases, ensuring that the rhubarb is distributed evenly between them, and bake for 30 minutes or until cooked through.

Yorkshire Rhubarb and Ginger Muffins

Makes 8

50ml Yorkshire Rapeseed Oil with Ginger
100ml milk
200g rhubarb (about 1 stem) cut i
nto 1cm chunks
125g golden caster sugar
1 large egg
175g plain flour
½ tsp baking powder
½ tsp bicarbonate of soda

104

Asparagus is one of the great British treats. It only has a short season though, so indulge whilst it's here!

Preheat the oven to 180°C / Fan 160°C / Gas mark 4

Trim and wash the asparagus, dry well and then toss it in a bowl with a little of the Oak Smoked Yorkshire Rapeseed Oil until it is all coated. Remove from the bowl and spread it out in a single layer on a baking tray, making sure there is no excess oil with the asparagus spears or they will become greasy as they cook.

Cook in the oven for about 4 minutes - be sure to keep an eye on the asparagus as it cooks very quickly!

Meanwhile, fry one egg for each person in Oak Smoked Yorkshire Rapeseed Oil, leaving the yolk soft enough to dip the asparagus spears into.

Serve the egg and asparagus spears with a sprinkling of sea salt and freshly ground black pepper.

Try this...
* Cook the asparagus in **Yorkshire Rapeseed Oil with Basil** and fry the egg using our regular **Yorkshire Rapeseed Oil.**
* Choose your favourite **Yorkshire Mayonnaise** as a dipping alternative to the egg.

Roasted Asparagus with Fried Egg Dipper

Oak Smoked Yorkshire Rapeseed Oil
Fresh British asparagus
One organic free range egg per person
Salt and black pepper

Preheat the oven to 200°C / Fan 180°C / Gas Mark 6

Tear up the bread and put it in a food processer, blitz until rough breadcrumbs have started to form. Add the Oak Smoked Yorkshire Rapeseed Oil, garlic and seasoning and blend further until all the ingredients are combined.

Place the chicken breasts in an oven proof dish and, using your hands, press the breadcrumb mixture onto each piece until they are all covered. Bake in the oven for 30 minutes.

After 30 minutes remove the chicken from the oven and lay the asparagus and tomatoes in the dish alongside the chicken. Drizzle a touch more of the Oak Smoked Yorkshire Rapeseed Oil over the vegetables and return to the oven for a further 7-10 minutes until the asparagus is cooked (be sure not to let it over cook).

We like to serve this with new potatoes tossed in our **Mint and Balsamic Dressing.**

Try this...
* **Chicken with Lemon Breadcrumb Crust** - Make the breadcrumb crust in the same way, using 6 tbsp **Yorkshire Mayonnaise with Lemon**, 100g fresh breadcrumbs, 2 tsp dried thyme, 2 tbsp sunflower seeds and 80g grated parmesan cheese. Cook for 30 - 40 minutes until the topping is golden and the chicken is cooked through. This works equally well with our **Natural or Garlic Mayonnaise**
* **Salmon with Lemon Breadcrumb Crust** - simply use salmon instead of chicken!

Baked Chicken with a Smoked Crumb Crust

Serves 4

120ml Oak Smoked Yorkshire Rapeseed Oil - plus extra for drizzling
4 large skinless chicken breasts
160g seeded or white bread (4 slices)
2 cloves garlic, peeled and chopped
Salt and black pepper
2 bundles fresh British asparagus
24 cherry tomatoes on the vine

Cut the beetroot into chunks, break the walnuts into smaller pieces and put all the ingredients into a food processor to combine. The texture shouldn't be too smooth, it's good to have the crunchiness of the walnuts in this dip.

Turn into a serving dish and drizzle a little Oak Smoked Yorkshire Rapeseed Oil on top to finish. Serve with strips of **Flatbread** to dip!

Beetroot and Walnut Dip

2 tbsp Oak Smoked Yorkshire Rapeseed Oil
225g cooked beetroot, skins removed
50g walnuts
50g wholemeal breadcrumbs
3 tsp hot horseradish sauce

Great as a side dish or in the centre of a salad. We've used our Oak Smoked Yorkshire Rapeseed Oil for this recipe, but it will work with any of our Deli Oils or Dressings Range.

Couscous Stuffed Peppers

Preheat the oven to 200°C / Fan 180°C / Gas Mark 6

Cut a lid off each of the peppers and hollow them out, removing the seeds. Place to one side ready for filling.

Prepare the couscous according to the instructions on the packet. When all the water has been absorbed, separate and fluff up the grains using a fork.

Heat 1 tbsp of the Oak Smoked Yorkshire Rapeseed Oil in a small pan over a medium heat on the hob and lightly fry the onion and mushrooms until soft. Remove from the hob and add to the couscous, making sure any excess juices remain in the pan as you don't want the couscous to become too wet.

Stir through, adding the cheese and remaining 1 tbsp Oak Smoked Yorkshire Rapeseed Oil. Season well and have a taste, you can add more oil, or juices from the pan if needed.

Spoon the couscous into the peppers and put their lids back on. Place in the oven and roast for 20-25 minutes, making sure the peppers are cooked, but do not brown.

A good tip is to place your peppers in a muffin or bun tray to roast them, it will help them to stay upright!

Makes 2

2 tbsp Oak Smoked Yorkshire Rapeseed Oil
2 medium red peppers
70g couscous
½ onion, peeled and chopped
2 mushrooms, chopped
Salt and pepper
40g Wensleydale cheese

Yorkshire Rapeseed Oil Dressings

All our dressing are made from home developed recipes, tried and tested in our own farm kitchen. They are all made by combining our own Yorkshire Rapeseed Oil with the finest ingredients.

Honey and Mustard

Awarded One Gold Star at the 2013 Great Taste Awards, this is our Yorkshire take on a classic dressing that will brighten up any salad. Alternatively brush onto chicken or parsnips before roasting.

Mint and Balsamic

Fabulous drizzled on hot or cold new potatoes, or great as an accompaniment or marinade for roast lamb. Try it on a feta and couscous salad, or even on fresh strawberries!

Smoked Chilli

A smoky, spicy dressing guaranteed to wake up any dish! A fantastic marinade for chicken and prawns, ideal for BBQ season, or wake up your winter pasta sauce, pizza or soup with a little drizzle, or for the spice friendly straight on to your salad.

Fennel Seed

This delicious dressing is the closest to a vinaigrette within our range. Beautiful when used with fish and pork, or stirred through rice and couscous. A strong flavour that lends itself to all seasons

Dijon and Black Pepper

This wonderfully versatile dressing is ideal as a salad dressing, but equally tempting as a stir-fry sauce or as an ingredient for your slow roasted beef.

Chicken Skewers

Cut the chicken pieces into 4cm chunks, push onto the wooden kebab sticks and lay them on a baking tray. Brush the chicken with Honey and Mustard Dressing, turning the kebab sticks until all the chicken is covered.

Cover with cling film and leave in the fridge for 30 minutes, then repeat.

Cook on a barbecue, griddle pan or in an oven preheated to 180°C / Fan 160°C / Gas Mark 4.

Honey and Mustard Dressing
Chicken breasts
Wooden kebab sticks

Celery, Cauliflower, Apple and Raisin Salad

Cut the cauliflower into very small florets. Cut the apples into quarters, remove the core and then cut into pieces roughly 1cm in size. Cut the celery into slices about 5mm thick

Mix the Honey and Mustard Dressing with the yogurt in a large bowl, add the cauliflower, apple, celery and raisins and mix well.

Leave in the fridge for at least an hour before serving.

2 tbsp Honey and Mustard Dressing
3 tbsp natural low fat yogurt
$1/2$ a small cauliflower
2 eating apples
4 sticks celery
50g raisins

Pear, Pecan and Yorkshire Blue Cheese Salad

Cut the pears into quarters, remove the core and then cut into pieces roughly 1cm in size. Break the pecan nuts in half. Cut the cheese into small cubes.

Combine the Honey and Mustard Dressing and the peanut butter in a bowl.

Add the pears, nuts and cheese and mix well before serving.

Alternatively serve the dressing in a small bowl alongside the salad.

3 tbsp Honey and Mustard Dressing
2 tsp crunchy peanut butter
2 large pears
50g pecan nuts
75g Yorkshire Blue cheese

Preheat the oven to 180°C / Fan 160°C / Gas Mark 4

To make the Honey and Mustard Mash peel and boil the potatoes until cooked, drain and mash, adding 2 tbsp of the Honey and Mustard Dressing.

To make the cheese sauce place 3 tbsp Yorkshire Rapeseed Oil in a non-stick pan over a low heat. Add the flour gradually, stirring all the while. Take off the heat and stir in the milk a little at a time to avoid creating lumps. Place back onto the hob over a medium heat, bring to the boil slowly, stirring continuously, until the sauce thickens. Turn the heat down to low, add the cheese and stir until it has all melted into the sauce. Finally add the remaining 2 tbsp Honey and Mustard Dressing and mix well.

To complete the dish place the cooked, mixed vegetable into a large ovenproof dish. Cover with the cheese sauce and mix together well. Top with the mashed potato and brush the top with Honey and Mustard Dressing. Place in the centre of the oven and cook for 30 minutes, until the vegetables are heated through and the top begins to brown.

Try this...
 * **Fish Pie with Honey and Mustard Mash** - use fish instead of mixed vegetables, a mixture of salmon, cod, smoked haddock, prawns... whatever is available and takes your fancy!
 * The mash topping makes excellent **Honey and Mustard Potato Cakes.**

Vegetable Bake with Honey and Mustard Mash

Serves 4

4 tbsp Honey & Mustard Dressing plus extra for brushing over the top
3 tbsp Yorkshire Rapeseed Oil
1kg vegetables, prepared and cooked weight
850g potatoes
75g plain flour
550ml milk
175g cheddar cheese, grated

You can use almost any vegetables for this quick and easy vegetarian dish, a mixture of colours and textures makes a good combination. Either prepare and cook the vegetables specifically for this recipe, or it's a tasty way to use up left overs.

Combine all the ingredients except the flour in a bowl and mix together well. Once mixed, use your hands to form cake shapes with the mixture. Dip each cake into the bowl of flour to coat and set aside until all the mixture is used. This should make about 6 potato cakes.

Heat a little Yorkshire Rapeseed Oil in a frying pan and, when the pan is hot, place in the cakes. Cook on each side for a few minutes until golden brown. Either serve immediately or keep in a hot oven for up to 10 minutes until needed.

These are great to make in advance and keep in the fridge, then just fry when needed.

Cheesy Potato Cakes

Makes 6

2 tbsp Honey and Mustard Dressing
600g mashed potato
75g grated mature cheddar
2 slices of ham shredded into small pieces (optional)
½ onion, peeled and grated
A good pinch of salt and pepper
A bowl of plain flour for coating

An easy side dish that can be made with a variety of our dressings or deli oils.

**Mint and Balsamic Dressing
or Dressing / Deli Oil of your choice**
Courgettes
Peppers
Aubergines
Fennel Bulbs

Slice the courgettes lengthways into thin strips.
Slice the aubergines into rounds.
Cut the peppers into quarters and remove the seeds.
Slice the fennel into rounds.

Using a pastry brush, coat the vegetables on one side with your desired dressing or oil; the recipe works equally well with Fennel Seed Dressing or Dijon and Black Pepper Dressing.

Leave the vegetables for about 5 minutes to absorb the dressing then turn them over and repeat on the other side.

Heat a griddle pan over high heat on the hob and, when the pan is hot, lay strips of vegetables in it, ensuring they don't overlap. Cook for a few minutes until they begin to have dark griddle marks on them, then turn and cook on the other side in the same way.

Once cooked through turn out onto a plate and serve immediately.

Try this...
* **Courgette and Feta Wraps**- wrap strips of griddled courgette around pieces of feta cheese with small strips of griddled peppers for bite size finger food.

Greek Style Couscous Salad

This salad makes a great light lunch or is fantastic served with lamb chops straight off the barbecue.

Makes one large dinner party size bowl

100ml Mint and Balsamic Dressing
250g couscous
100g Kalamata olives
½ cucumber, cut into 1cm cubes
1 packet of Feta cheese
1 red onion, peeled and finely sliced

Prepare the couscous according to the instructions on the packet. When all the water has been absorbed, separate and fluff up the grains using a fork.

Once the couscous is cold crumble in the feta cheese and add the cucumber, onion and olives, mixing thoroughly. Pour in the Mint and Balsamic Dressing and mix well.

Chill in the fridge until ready to serve.

Preheat the oven to 180°C / Fan 160°C / Gas Mark 4

Cut the lamb steaks into cubes about 3cm in size. Heat the Yorkshire Rapeseed Oil with Mixed Herbs over a high heat in a heavy based pan which has a lid. Add the onion and fry until translucent. Add the garlic and lamb and fry until the lamb has browned all over, stirring and turning constantly. Roughly chop the tomato after removing the seeds and skin (see page 51) and add to the pan. Mix everything together well.

Put the lid on, turn the hob down to its lowest setting and cook for one hour, stirring occasionally.

Using a slotted spoon, remove the lamb and vegetables from the pan and put them into a bowl. Add the Mint and Balsamic Dressing to the juices left in the pan, turn the heat up and boil to reduce the liquid to about 2-3 tbsp. Remove from the hob and pour over the lamb and vegetables. Leave to cool.

Crumble the feta cheese into a bowl.

When the lamb and vegetables are cool, take the filo pastry, one sheet at a time, to make the parcels. Filo pastry dries out very quickly, so keep the sheets you're not using under a damp cloth.

Place a sheet of pastry on a work surface and brush it all over with a thin coating of Yorkshire Rapeseed Oil. Fold the pastry in half along its long edge to make an oblong.

Place a quarter of the feta cheese in the centre of the pastry, then a quarter of the lamb mixture on top of the cheese, together with some of the vegetables and juices. Brush all round with Yorkshire Rapeseed Oil. Fold the top down over the lamb mixture and then fold the sides in towards the middle.

Now roll the parcel up, place it on a baking tray and brush the top with Yorkshire Rapeseed Oil. Repeat this to make the remaining three parcels.

Cook in the oven for 25 - 30 minutes until the pastry is golden and crispy.

Mix all the ingredients, except the flour, together in a bowl until thoroughly combined. Divide into eight and mould into patties. Put the flour into a bowl and dip each potato cake in to coat it with flour.

Heat a little Yorkshire Rapeseed Oil in a pan and fry the cakes over a high heat for 3-4 minutes on each side until brown and crispy.

Serve as part of a meal or on their own with **Yorkshire Mayonnaise with Garlic!**

Lamb and Feta Filo Parcels

Makes 4

1 tsp Mint and Balsamic Dressing
1 tbsp Yorkshire Rapeseed Oil with Mixed Herbs
Yorkshire Rapeseed Oil
400g leg of British lamb steaks
1 onion, peeled and sliced
4 tomatoes, skins and seeds removed (see page 51)
1 clove of garlic, peeled and chopped
200gm Feta cheese
Salt and black pepper
4 sheets of filo pastry

Pea and Mint Potato Cakes

Makes 8

2½ tbsp Mint and Balsamic Dressing
Yorkshire Rapeseed Oil for frying
500g mashed potato
150g cooked peas
Salt and black pepper to season
100g plain flour

Prepare the fruit and mix it together in a bowl. Mix the Mint and Balsamic Dressing with the orange juice and add to the fruit mixture. Leave in the fridge to marinade for at least one hour before serving, garnished with a sprig of fresh mint.

Salad of Summer Fruits

For each person you will need
1 tsp Mint and Balsamic Dressing
2 tsp fresh orange juice
200g summer fruits
(we have used strawberries, blueberries and melon)
Fresh mint to garnish

If you grow courgettes, you'll know that they seem to have a will of their own. One minute they are tender young things on the plant, barely much larger than your finger, and then suddenly they have become ten times the size almost overnight! This is a good way to use up those larger courgettes. The recipe makes a large pan full so halve the quantities if you prefer to make less.

Courgette and Mint Soup

Serves 8

3 tbsp Yorkshire Rapeseed Oil
4 tbsp Mint and Balsamic Dressing
850g courgettes, tops and tails removed, sliced and diced
2 large onions, peeled and chopped
1 litre hot vegetable stock
60g long grain rice
Salt and black pepper

Fry the onions in the Yorkshire Rapeseed Oil in a large pan over a medium heat until soft, then add the courgettes and stir to mix well. Put the lid on the pan, turn the heat down to low and cook for a further 15 minutes so that the vegetables can release their juices.

Then add the vegetable stock, the Mint and Balsamic Dressing and rice. Stir well, bring to the boil and simmer over a low heat with the lid on for 30 minutes.

Blitz/liquidise and season with salt and pepper to suit your taste before serving.

Minted Yogurt

2 tbsp Mint and Balsamic Dressing
200ml natural Greek yogurt

So simple, yet so versatile! Serve as an accompaniment or as a dip, delicious either way.

Mix well and serve!
What could be more simple?

Try this...
Add some grated **cucumber** for a crispy texture.

121

Simon Barrett
The Chilli Jam Man

www.thechillijamman.com

> *"Our paths first crossed with Simon Barrett, known to most as 'The Chilli Jam Man', at York Festival of Food and Drink. Adam excitedly arrived home with a selection of jams for us to play with, the idea being that we could collaborate and create an exciting new product. A few years on, Simon now lives in Thixendale just across the road from us and shares our production premises. We are delighted that he uses our oils within some of his own product range and we, of course, would not have our 'Smoked Chilli Dressing' without him!"* Jennie Palmer.

Pre heat the oven to 200°C / Fan 180°C / Gas Mark 6

Rub the chicken breasts with the Smoked Chilli Dressing and leave in a dish to marinate for at least 1 hour.

Drizzle the Yorkshire Rapeseed Oil over the mushrooms and place in the oven to bake. Remove the mushrooms from the oven when cooked and keep them warm.

Meanwhile, heat a griddle pan on the hob, when hot remove the chicken from the dish, place in the pan with any remaining marinade and cook for a few minutes before turning, allowing the Smoked Chilli Dressing to caramelise onto the meat. If needed, drizzle a little Yorkshire Rapeseed Oil into the pan to aid cooking.

When the chicken is close to being cooked through, add the halloumi slices to the pan and cook for 2 minutes on each side. Make sure the halloumi is heated through, but be careful not to overcook it.

When these ingredients are cooked through, remove them from the pan and slice the chicken.

Then slice the muffin in half and toast each piece on both sides.

Start your stack with a piece of toasted muffin, then the mushroom, avocado, halloumi and finally the chicken. Drizzle over any remaining juices from the pan. A fantastic lunch!

Chicken and Halloumi Stack

Serves 2

4 tbsp Smoked Chilli Dressing
A drizzle of Yorkshire Rapeseed Oil
1 muffin
2 skinless chicken breasts
2 portobello mushrooms
1 avocado peeled, stoned and sliced
250g (1pack) Halloumi cheese, sliced

123

This is such an easy dish, a great lunch or supper that can be enjoyed throughout the seasons. Adjust the amount of Smoked Chilli Dressing to suit your taste.

King Prawn and Roasted Tomato Tagliatelle

Serves 4

2 tbsp Yorkshire Rapeseed Oil
4 tbsp Smoked Chilli Dressing
900g tomatoes, halved
1 large onion, peeled and finely chopped
4 cloves of garlic, peeled and chopped
400g King Prawns, cooked and peeled
Salt and black pepper
300g tagliatelle

Preheat the oven to 180°C / Fan 160°C / Gas Mark 4

Place the tomatoes, half the onion and the garlic in a roasting dish. Drizzle over half the Yorkshire Rapeseed Oil and season with the salt and pepper. Place in the oven and cook for 30 minutes until the tomatoes are soft and cooked through.

When cooked, remove from the oven and blend / blitz until smooth. Now add the Smoked Chilli Dressing according to your taste and put to one side.

Cook the tagliatelle in boiling water according to the instructions on the packet. Drain in a colander when cooked.

Meanwhile, heat the remaining oil in a large pan on the hob. Fry the remaining onions over a high heat for a few minutes until they start to soften, then add the prawns. Continue to fry until the prawns are heated through. Now add the tomato mixture and then the cooked tagliatelle.

Stir carefully to mix thoroughly. Serve with grated parmesan and a scattering of chopped fresh basil.

126

Roast Cod with Crispy Bacon

Serves 4

4 tbsp Smoked Chilli Dressing
2 tbsp Yorkshire Rapeseed Oil with Garlic
4 cod fillets
4 rashers streaky bacon, cut into thin strips
2 tbsp tomato purée
4 medium sized potatoes
1 large onion, peeled and chopped

Preheat the oven to 180°C / Fan 160°C / Gas Mark 4

Peel the potatoes and cut into 2cm cubes. Place them in a pan of cold water, bring to the boil and simmer for just 4 minutes and then drain.

Heat the Yorkshire Rapeseed Oil with Garlic in a frying pan, add the drained potato, chopped onion and bacon strips. Fry over a high heat, turning frequently, until the potatoes are cooked through and the bacon is crispy.

Lay the fillets of fish in an ovenproof dish. Mix the tomato purée and Smoked Chilli Dressing together to a paste and spread it over the top of the fish. Scatter the potato, onion and bacon mixture around the fish, cover with a lid or foil and bake in the oven for 20 minutes.

Remove the lid/foil, turn the oven up to 200°C / Fan 180°C / Gas Mark 6 and cook for a further 15 - 20 minutes.

Crab Cakes with Cucumber and Mint Garnish

Makes 8

2-3 tsp Smoked Chilli Dressing
Yorkshire Rapeseed Oil for frying
3 tbsp cream cheese
100g white crab meat
200g cooked and crushed new potatoes, skins removed
2 spring onions, finely sliced
2 tsp fresh coriander, roughly chopped
Fine oatmeal for coating
Cucumber slices

Mix the cream cheese and Smoked Chilli Dressing together in a bowl, add the crab meat and potatoes, spring onions and coriander and mix everything together well.

Divide the mixture into 8 equal portions and shape each one into a ball, then flatten slightly into a small crab cake. Coat each crab cake in fine oatmeal.

Heat enough Yorkshire Rapeseed Oil in a frying pan to just cover the surface, then fry the crab cakes over a moderate heat for a few minutes on each side until golden brown.

Serve on a bed of thinly sliced cucumber marinated in **Mint Balsamic Dressing.**

127

Put the French beans and Yorkshire Rapeseed Oil in a bowl and mix together to thoroughly coat the beans with the oil. Heat a griddle pan on the hob and when hot, add the French beans and cook for about 3 minutes, or until cooked. Make sure they still have a bite to them, don't be tempted to overcook. Remove the beans from the pan and leave to cool.

In a large bowl, use your hands to mix together the rocket, spring onions, cheese if used and the cold cooked French beans.

Add the dressing of your choice and toss through. Turn out onto a serving dish and garnish with the Parma ham to serve.

Try this...
* For this recipe we like to use our Fennel Seed Dressing, but it is equally delicious with our **Honey and Mustard Dressing** or **Mint and Balsamic Dressing.**

French Bean and Rocket Salad

Serves 2-3 as a side dish

1 tbsp Yorkshire Rapeseed Oil
1 tbsp Fennel Seed Dressing
or Dressing of your choice
200g French beans
3 good handfuls wild rocket
4 slices Parma ham torn into strips
6 spring onions chopped
Wensleydale Cheese - optional

A crunchy, refreshing salad that's really easy to make!

Combine the Fennel Seed Dressing and lemon juice in a mixing bowl. Fold in the celeriac, apple and chopped fennel. Mix well and serve.

Celeriac, Apple and Fennel Salad

2 tbsp Fennel Seed Dressing
1 tbsp lemon juice
220g celeriac root - prepared weight, peeled, and cut into matchstick size pieces
2 green eating apples, quartered, cored and grated
2 tbsp feathery green fennel leaves, chopped

129

Pork Chops with Fennel and Apple

Serves 4

2 tbsp Yorkshire Rapeseed Oil with Black Pepper
4 tbsp Fennel Seed Dressing
4 British pork loin chops
4 medium sized potatoes
1 onion, peeled and sliced
1 large cooking apple, peeled, cored and sliced
1 fennel bulb, white part sliced, green feathery part retained for garnish
220ml vegetable stock
Salt and pepper to taste

The slight sharpness of the fennel and apple contrast well with the pork in this dish, which needs only fresh vegetables to accompany it – try shredded spring greens stir fried in a flavoured Yorkshire Rapeseed Oil of your choice.

Heat the oven to 180°C / Fan 160°C / Gas Mark 4

Peel the potatoes, cut into slices about 5mm thick and place in a pan with enough cold water to just cover. Bring to the boil, simmer for 3 minutes and drain carefully, to avoid breaking up the slices.

Heat the Yorkshire Rapeseed Oil with Black Pepper in a frying pan over a high heat on the hob and brown the chops on both sides. Remove the chops from the frying pan and keep them warm. Add the stock to the frying pan and bring to the boil, stirring in any meat juices, then remove from the heat.

In a large oven proof casserole dish, place layers of potato, onion, apple and fennel, season with a little salt and pepper between layers.

Pour in the hot stock. Place the chops on top of the apples and vegetables, in one layer.

Coat each chop with 1 tbsp Fennel Seed Dressing. Cover the casserole dish with a lid (or foil) and cook in the oven for 30 - 45 minutes depending on the thickness of the chops. After 15 minutes, turn the chops over in the casserole. Leave the lid off when you turn the chops over if you prefer them to brown and crisp up a little more.

Charred Pork Fillet

Serves 2

4tbsp Fennel Seed Dressing
400g British pork fillet
4 tbsp orange marmalade
Pinch of salt
Black pepper

In a bowl, combine the Fennel Seed Dressing with the marmalade and salt and pepper. Cut the pork fillet into smaller strips and lay them out, side by side like sardines. Push kebab skewers through each section of the fillet, evenly spaced with 1cm gap between each piece of fillet, so that you end up with a square of pork.

Marinade the pork in the dressing glaze for a few hours (or overnight if you have time).

To cook, place the pork under a hot grill, (with a tray underneath),

and cook each side for 10 minutes or until golden brown. Re-apply any glaze you have left (or which has dripped into the tray) when you turn over the pork. Once cooked, cut the fillets parallel with the skewers to make even sized kebabs.

Add any leftover glaze from the tray to the kebab once it's on the plate. Serve with a generous pile of **Coleslaw** and **Flatbread**.

Preheat the oven to 200°C / Fan 180°C / Gas Mark 6

Line a baking tray with baking paper.

Slice the leek lengthways and then thinly slice across each piece, wash and drain well. Fry the leek gently in the Yorkshire Rapeseed Oil with Lemon over a moderate heat until it just starts to soften. Remove from the heat, put the leek into a mixing bowl and leave to cool.

When the leek is cold, add the precooked fish, soured cream and Fennel Seed Dressing. Season with salt and pepper to taste. Mix together gently and put to one side.

Now roll out the pastry and, cutting round a 7cm plate, make two circles of pastry. Place half of the fish mixture onto each circle. Using a pastry brush, dampen round the outside edge of each pastry circle with water. Fold the top over and seal the edges by crimping them together with your fingers.

Brush the top and sealed edge of each pasty with beaten egg, make a small hole in the top to release the steam and then bake in the oven for 20 minutes until the pastry is a rich, golden colour.

Try this...
* **Salmon and Leek Pasties**: you can use any fish of your choice for this dish. Try using salmon, it's readily available and goes really well with the leek and Fennel Seed Dressing.

Sea Bass and Leek Pasties

Makes 2

One quantity of pastry (see page 15)

2 tsp Fennel Seed Dressing
2 tsp Yorkshire Rapeseed Oil with Lemon
100g cooked sea bass, skin and bones removed
$1/_2$ a leek
2 tbsp soured cream
Salt and pepper
Beaten egg for glazing

Preheat the oven to 180°C / Fan 160°C / Gas Mark 4

Place the mushrooms stalk side up in an ovenproof dish.

Drizzle 1tsp Dijon and Black Pepper Dressing over each mushroom.

To make the stuffing, heat the Yorkshire Rapeseed Oil with Black Pepper in a pan over a medium heat on the hob. Add the spring onions and fry gently for a couple of minutes. Remove the pan from the heat, stir in the breadcrumbs and parsley plus half of the parmesan cheese. Combine all the ingredients and fill the mushrooms with the mixture.

Sprinkle the remaining parmesan over the top of each stuffed mushroom. Place in the oven and cook for about 20-25 minutes until the mushrooms are cooked and the topping has browned.

Stuffed Portobello Mushrooms

4 tsp Dijon and Black Pepper Dressing
1 tbsp Yorkshire Rapeseed Oil with Black Pepper
4 large Portobello mushrooms
50g fresh breadcrumbs
8 spring onions, roughly chopped
1 tbsp chopped fresh parsley
50g grated Parmesan cheese

135

Preheat the oven to 220°C / Fan 200°C / Gas Mark 7

Line a baking tray with baking paper.

Lay the pastry out on a lightly floured surface and cut it in half length ways. Using a pastry brush, spread a layer of the Dijon and Black Pepper Dressing over each piece of pastry. Then sprinkle the grated parmesan on top, followed by the prosciutto slices in a single layer.

Now fold the long outer edges of each piece of pastry into the centre, taking care to enclose all of the topping. Then fold in half length ways to create the palmier shape.

Using a sharp knife - or better still, a sharp pair of kitchen scissors - cut each length of pastry roll into slices about $\frac{1}{2}$ cm thick.

Place on a baking tray lined with baking paper and cook in the oven for 12-15 minutes until the palmiers are crisp and golden.

Remove from the oven and place the palmiers on a wire rack to cool, they're gorgeous served slightly warm!

Try this...
* Try using different Dressings - our **Smoked Chilli Dressing** goes well with grated cheddar cheese, or perhaps use **Basil and Pine Nut Pesto** with extra grated parmesan spread on top.

Savoury Palmiers

Dijon and Black Pepper Dressing
1 x 320g packet ready rolled puff pastry
6 slices prosciutto
40g grated parmesan

2 Mayo

DRIZZLE
ROAST
BAKE
FRY

Esther Palmer

Yorkshire Rapeseed Oil Mayonnaise

A great Yorkshire take on an old classic and a favourite for any Yorkshire dining table.

Yorkshire Mayonnaise

Our creamy Yorkshire Mayonnaise is made using our Award winning cold pressed Yorkshire Rapeseed Oil, free range egg and just a touch of mustard. A delicious choice for your salads, chips and much, much more.

Yorkshire Mayonnaise with Lemon

Made with our popular Yorkshire Rapeseed Oil with Lemon, this Mayonnaise promises to liven up any salad! Beautiful with prawns, chicken, avocado......

Yorkshire Mayonnaise with Garlic

Made using our best selling Yorkshire Rapeseed Oil with Garlic, this product offers a twist to the classic alternative. Great with what ever you fancy. Garlic lovers - this one is for you!

Images by Jason Lowe

James Mackenzie
The Pipe & Glass Inn

www.pipeandglass.co.uk

Fishcakes can be old hat, but everyone loves them. You can use any kind of fish you like: I like to use a lot of fish, so really you are just using the potato to bind it. Pollock works really well and it's not too expensive. It's great to make your own Tartare Sauce, as you can make it nice and chunky with Yorkshire Mayonnaise.

Bake the potatoes in the oven and scrape out the flesh from the skin; this way you will end up with a nice dry fishcake. Skin and de-bone the Pollock fillets, lay them on an oiled baking sheet and bake in the oven at 180°C / Fan 160°C / gas mark 4, until just cooked. Place the fish and potato in a large mixing bowl.

Chop the onion really finely, put into a saucepan with the white wine and zest and juice of the lemon. Cook the onions for 1 hour over a low to medium heat: by this time all the liquid should have been soaked up by the onions, but if not increase the heat until the mixture is as dry as possible. Cool and add to the fish and potatoes. This mixture will give the fishcakes a great sharpness.

Add a handful of breadcrumbs to the mix, some chopped parsley, dill and a little curry powder - this is not to spice it up but just adds a different flavour: you just need a little or you'll over power the fish.

Mould the fishcakes and cool in the fridge. When cool pass them through the flour, egg and breadcrumb and keep in the fridge until needed.

To pickle the samphire: bring 200ml of white wine vinegar to the boil with some pink peppercorns and sliced shallot, pour over the samphire and leave for at least 2 hours. This is best after a couple of days and will keep for ages; I tend to pickle it when the season is coming to an end so we can use it through the coming months.

For the homemade Tartare Sauce: roughly chop the cornichons and capers. Season with a little salt and a squeeze of lemon. Mix with the Yorkshire Mayonnaise, Dijon mustard and white wine vinegar. Chop some flat leaf parsley and add to the sauce.

Deep fry the fishcakes in Yorkshire Rapeseed Oil until golden brown and finish in the oven to cook them through.

Serve with the Tartare Sauce and some of the pickled samphire mixed through some salad leaves.

Pollock Fishcakes with homemade Tartare Sauce and Pickled Samphire

For the Pollock Fishcakes

1kg Maris Piper potatoes
1kg pollock
2 white onions
1 lemon
200ml white wine
Flat leaf parsley
Bunch of dill
Mild curry powder

Fresh white breadcrumbs
Plain flour
4 eggs
Yorkshire Rapeseed Oil for deep frying

For the Tartare Sauce
6 tbsp Yorkshire Mayonnaise
1 tbsp Dijon mustard
2 tbsp white wine vinegar
12 small cornichons
4 tbsp capers

For the Pickled Samphire
200g fresh samphire
1 tbsp pink peppercorns
2 shallots
200ml white wine vinegar

GUEST RECIPE

141

This is such a lovely meal to create, especially when our lovely local wet fish shop does all the preparation!

You'll usually find a good selection of ready prepared fresh shell fish during the summer months in the best supermarkets too.

Serve with your favourite **Yorkshire Mayonnaise** along with a glass or two of something cold and refreshing for a wonderfully relaxing summer treat!

Summer Shell Fish Platter

Our Yorkshire Mayonnaise with Lemon is a marriage made in heaven for shell fish!

Slice the bread across into two and toast each piece on the cut side.

Slice the chicken across to make two thin fillets and brush them with Smoked Chilli Dressing.

Heat a griddle pan on a high hob and cook the chicken fillets on both sides until brown and cooked through.

Mix the Yorkshire Mayonnaise with the Smoked Chilli Dressing and spread it over one of the ciabatta slices. Then place the cooked chicken fillets on top.

Serve the other slice of toasted ciabatta topped with **Marinated Peppers**, accompanied by a small bowl of **Chilli Salsa**.

And if you're feeling hungry, add some **Twice Fried Chips** too!

Smoked Chilli Chicken on Ciabatta

Serves One

For each person you will need:
1 tbsp Yorkshire Mayonnaise
2 tsp Smoked Chilli Dressing plus extra for griddling the chicken
1 skinless chicken breast
Ciabatta bread, a piece about 8cm long

A really flavoursome dressing that will keep in the fridge for a few days after making.

Combine all the ingredients, excluding the Yorkshire Rapeseed Oil, in a bowl and blend with a hand blender until smooth.

Continuing to blend, drizzle in the Yorkshire Rapeseed Oil until all the ingredients are blended in a dressing-like consistency.

Yorkshire Caesar Dressing

4 tbsp Yorkshire Mayonnaise
100ml Yorkshire Rapeseed Oil
1 clove garlic, peeled and crushed
30g grated Parmesan cheese
3 anchovy fillets
2 tbsp lemon juice
2 tsp Worcestershire sauce

Carefully shell and halve the boiled eggs and scoop the yolk out into a bowl. With a fork, break up the yolks and blend in the Yorkshire Mayonnaise and a few twists of black pepper. Spoon the mayo/yolk mixture back into the egg white halves. Top with a twist of black pepper and serve immediately.

Try this...
Use our **Yorkshire Mayonnaise with Garlic** for something a little different.

Yorkshire Egg Mayonnaise

Yorkshire Mayonnaise
1½ tsp per egg used
Boiled eggs, as many as you require
Black pepper

Simply mix chunks of avocado with equal quantities of shelled prawns and combine with generous amounts of Yorkshire Mayonnaise with Garlic.

Serve on a bed of finely shredded lettuce.

Prawn and Avocado Salad

Yorkshire Mayonnaise with Garlic
Prawns, shelled and cooked
Avocado, peeled and stone removed
Lettuce

Finely slice or grate all the ingredients into a large bowl. Add the Yorkshire Mayonnaise with Garlic, horseradish sauce and the salt and pepper. If you like it a bit looser add more mayo and horseradish sauce.

Seasonal Greens Coleslaw

2 tbsp Yorkshire Mayonnaise with Garlic
2 tbsp Horseradish sauce
$^1/_4$ white cabbage, finely sliced
$^1/_2$ red onion, peeled and coarsely grated
2 carrots, peeled and coarsely grated
A handful of collard greens or spring cabbage, washed and spun dry
2 crunchy apples, very finely sliced
Sea salt and freshly ground black pepper

Yorkshire Tapas

Ideas to inspire you!

Below: Mini flatbread wraps with prosciutto and chilli salsa; tiny chorizo meat balls with halloumi and marinated peppers; baby tomatoes stuffed with cream cheese mixed with Smoked Chilli Dressing on a crispy chorizo slice.

Bottom: Toast brushed with Oak Smoked Oil and topped with beetroot and walnut dip; toast brushed with Basil Oil and topped with basil and tomato salsa; toast brushed with Lemon Oil and topped with white crab meat mixed with Lemon Mayonnaise.

Left to right: Yorkshire quails' egg mayonnaise; mini parmesan baskets filled with smoked salmon rolled with cream cheese and Fennel Seed Dressing; prawn and avocado salad with Garlic Mayonnaise.

Index

A

B

V

W

Y

All Yorkshire Rapeseed Oil products can be ordered online at **www.yorkshirerapeseedoil.co.uk** or see our website for details of our stockists and the markets we'll be attending.

Conversion Chart

Different conversion charts have slightly different details as generally the figures have been either rounded up or down slightly to give whole amounts. Most kitchen scales offer a metric or imperial option, whichever you decide to use, be sure not to mix the two in the same recipe.

Weights

25g = 1oz

110g = 4oz

225g = 8oz

450g = 1lb

Volume

30ml = 1 fl oz

150ml = 5 fl oz / ¼ pint

600ml = 20 fl oz / 1 pint

Dimensions

1 cm = ½ inch

2.5 cm = 1 inch

6cm = 2½ inches

10cm = 4 inches

20 cm = 8 inches

Oven Temperatures

°C	Fan °C	°F	Gas Mark
130°C	= 110°C fan	= 250°F	= Gas mark 1
150°C	= 130°C fan	= 300°F	= Gas mark 2
170°C	= 150°C fan	= 325°F	= Gas mark 3
180°C	= 160°C fan	= 350°F	= Gas mark 4
190°C	= 170°C fan	= 375°F	= Gas mark 5
200°C	= 180°C fan	= 400°F	= Gas mark 6
220°C	= 200°C fan	= 425°F	= Gas mark 7
230°C	= 210°C fan	= 450°F	= Gas mark 8
240°C	= 220°C fan	= 475°F	= Gas mark 9